The Seven-Minute Millionaire
HOW TO THINK YOURSELF RICH

Be sure to visit the web site for free tips and reports on retiring
rich, business ideas, creating wealth and more.

www.the7minutemillionaire.com

The Seven-Minute Millionaire
HOW TO THINK YOURSELF RICH

TONY NEUMEYER

WALKING CROW

The Seven-Minute Millionaire: How To Think Yourself Rich

Published by Walking Crow
First edition

Walking Crow
363-1350 Burrard Street
Vancouver, BC V6Z 0C2
Canada

www.the7minutemillionaire.com

Cataloguing data available from Library and Archives Canada

ISBN 978-0-9938648-0-3
eBook ISBN 978-0-9938648-1-0

Editing by Kate Unrau and Michelle MacAleese
Cover design by Peter Cocking
Text design by WildElement.ca
Photography by Michelle Neumeyer
Printed in Canada

To my mother, for helping program my mind with the fact that I could be a success at whatever I set my mind to and for providing my brothers and me with a very good home despite some difficult circumstances.

To my wife, Michelle, for encouraging me to write my thoughts and share them with the world.

To my son, Justin, and daughter, Kristi, hoping that I have instilled in them the sense and knowledge that they can be and do whatever they set their minds to.

To my brother Keith, for providing me with business insight and opportunities along the way.

To my brother David, for being himself.

The greater danger for most of us lies not in

setting our aim too high and falling short; but in

setting our aim low, and achieving our mark.

Michelangelo

CONTENTS

ACKNOWLEDGMENTS

I would like to thank John Aarons for his friendship and ongoing assistance, insight and direction for the many writings to which he has given input over the years. I would also like to thank the author Gina Woolsey, who gave me excellent insights into publishing and sent me in the right direction for creating a book that I hope will be highly useful for those who read it and choose to implement these strategies. Also, thank you to Trena White of Page Two Strategies, for her excellent publishing advice, introduction to contacts, and industry knowledge.

PREFACE

I first thought about writing this book some time ago, but I realized that I should only write it if it would bring value to others. I sat on the idea for a while so I could really focus on the best way I could help people – and when I say help people, I don't just mean in some vague way that may transpire into something better. No! I mean showing people how to have concrete goals and giving them tried and tested strategies to attain those goals and dreams.

By the age of ten, I'd already told my mother that I was going to be rich. Our family didn't have any money at that time; in fact, my mom was pretty much broke. She had me when she was only sixteen years old, and by the time I was four, she and my dad had split up. We were on our own – me, my two brothers, and my mother. She suffered a lot of hardship, we all did as my dad was not contributing or helping out, but to be fair, he was young also. At one point my mother actually felt it was in our best interest be raised by someone with the means to do so, so she put us in a foster home. We three boys were split up into different homes, but my mom couldn't handle it and it was only a few days before she claimed us back and we started our life's journey together. One Thanksgiving Day, we received our meal from the Salvation Army. Although I was able to go to summer camp, it was only because my mother was able to muster up the nerve to talk with the people at the YMCA and apply for a full subsidy. OK, going to camp may not sound like hardship, but my Mom did it so we would have the experience of such a setting (it was very basic) and to keep us from following other kids down the wrong path. I won't go into all the details, but there was no silver spoon. Our lives were filled with tough times, but we managed through it because we helped each other, as families do. Eventually, despite her rocky start in life, my mother became a great success in the real estate industry, as did I.

My mother always told us kids that we could do anything, be anyone, and accomplish anything we set out to do. It was because of her continued optimism and guidance during our early years that we believed this. That's not to say we didn't have failures along the way; that would just be unrealistic. Mom gave my brothers and me the "room" to fail, but she always said, it's OK, just get "back on that horse" and do it until you succeed, but learn from what you have done previously.

I've had many failures. When I was twenty-one years old, I had progressed into selling real estate, and soon after that I moved into real estate development. About a year later, the real estate market collapsed and I was left holding a lot of real estate that I couldn't sell. I ended up over 1.5 million dollars in debt even after everything had been sold, and I had no way of paying it back.

As I'm sure you can imagine, that was a very difficult time for me personally. I spent most of my time feeling stressed and worried. A lot of people would say that money isn't that important and that other things should take priority, but let me tell you, when you're down and out, you have no income, and you owe more than 1.5 million dollars . . . all of a sudden, money *is* important. It wasn't just knowing that I had to find a way to put food on the table; it was bankers, the mortgage company, and the suppliers all telling me that money is important. They wanted their money, and they wanted it pretty damn quick! I was receiving so many summons from the courts that I actually got to know the bailiff by his first name.

How did all this happen? When times were good, I'd purchased three properties, putting no money down. When the market collapsed, I was in the process of selling a building lot, building a luxury home in an expensive area of Vancouver, and renovating another home. The time had been right to take a chance – or so I had thought – and though I had no experience in developing, I had brought in a builder to do the construction part of the different jobs. I was mortgaged to within an inch of my life: three mortgages and lines of credit against the properties. When they were eventually sold during this rapidly declining market, I was deep in debt – like I said, over a million and a half dollars. I ended up declaring personal and corporate bankruptcy.

It was clear to me that I had to do something to start bringing some money back in. The idea of owing money was not on my radar, and it had been difficult for me to come to terms with. In her younger years, my mother had been a salesperson at a credit collection agency. She had instilled in us from an early age the idea that we should always pay our bills on time, and that we should make sure to stay out of debt. I imagine that many of you have been brought up the same way, so you can understand that it was a very traumatic time in my life. Chances are that some of you have also experienced being short of money and are seeking a way to make a better and brighter future.

One thing that bankruptcy did do for me was to make me a stronger and more determined person – one who would succeed, no matter what. I've developed a system to help you get there also. The method is so simple that anyone who puts their mind to it can use it to create whatever they desire in their life. It isn't hard to enhance the path you are on or change your direction to the one you want to take. It doesn't even take long! In fact, you can do it in a matter of weeks. As I formalized this strategy in my mind, I decided it was the right time to pass the knowledge onto others so that you too can enjoy a better future.

As you read the pages herein, I hope you will find it enjoyable as you realize that you have it in your power to control nearly everything in your life. The future is yours!

Motivation is what gets you started.

Habit is what keeps you going.

Jim Rohn

INTRODUCTION

In this book, you will find detailed descriptions of the principles that I've personally used to gain success in my life. I've earned millions of dollars selling real estate, investing, speculating, and building a business, so I do feel that I know what I'm talking about! I'm speaking from personal experience, and I'm going to share with you exactly what works. I will explain what I've done to get to where I am, and share the principles you can utilize to do whatever it is that you want to do in your life.

I'm not telling you of my success to impress you, but to impress *upon* you the significance of these principles. The idea that you are able to create whatever you want for your life seems almost magical . . . We've all dreamed a magical life for ourselves at some time, haven't we? For me, the dream became my reality, and I'll show you how to make your dream into your reality. I'm 100 percent confident that when you employ these principles, your level of success will improve, in the same way that mine did.

Not only am *I* living proof of how these techniques work, I have worked with many people who have used them to reach the highest levels of success in many sectors of life. Later in the book, I will bring to you some of the "other" empirical data, psychological and even new age practices that further validate the techniques and strategies I will talk about. Don't worry; I won't go too far down the esoteric road; that isn't really me. But I have found some quality evidence of how this process works and I think it's worth bringing this to your attention.

The theme of this book is the creation of large amounts of wealth in your life, but money is not the only kind of richness, so don't worry about it from that perspective. Money is your measuring stick, representing both success and freedom from worry. *The Seven-Minute Millionaire* isn't exclusively about money, but we are all aware of the freedom and comfort that money can buy for you.

I'm sure there are many other aspects of your life in which you want to make changes, and the simple techniques explained in this book are also going to help you with these: your relationships, your health, and even your sense of well-being. Whatever your aspirations for your life, you can get there with my techniques.

This is going to be all-encompassing and not just about money. Keep in mind that when you attain wealth, you also gain the ability to help a lot of people. For some, that's a significant aspect of success. It's not just what money can do for you, it's also what you can then do for others.

I've shared some quotes I love, however, my intention is not to motivate you in the usual sense. This is not a book of fluff or of generic statements because I find that kind of motivation is external and quickly fades. But if you use the techniques that I'm going to share with you, I hope you'll find yourself inspired and encouraged. These techniques will help you to train your brain, drawing you toward the success that you desire and need in your life. Unlike *The Law of Attraction*, this book goes far beyond theory, providing specific actions to create a seven-minute Personal Programming Message (PPM).

I have provided a number of my favorite quotes throughout the book and at the beginning of each chapter. These are there for a purpose, they are not filler. As you read each chapter you can think about the quote and how it relates to the content, and especially the exercises in each chapter.

This method isn't about working harder; it's about working smarter. The name, *The Seven-Minute Millionaire*, stems from a commitment to set aside just seven minutes in your life. Dedicate the time to creating the future you want for you and your family. Seven minutes' worth of messages can actually change the way your subconscious mind works for you. Seven minutes' worth of messages can draw success toward you.

Let me give you a quick explanation of this. The conscious mind is what we use every day to think and make decisions, while the subconscious mind is the part that works behind the scenes, coming up with ways to create what we think about in our conscious minds. It also protects us from being hurt or injured. If you think about it, we are constantly bombarded with messages, noises, distractions and elements every moment of every day. Our subconscious is receiving programming each and every day from external messages and the thoughts you have throughout your waking moments. But allowing those random thoughts and messages to set our course is not the way to achieve what you desire. The best way to create the future you want is to program your own personal computer, your subconscious, to take you where you want to go. That, is what this book shows you how to do.

You may find it helpful to have someone else using the strategies and techniques with you. Someone you can work with to implement the ideas in the book. Previously, I took part in a mentorship group where we worked collaboratively to help each other along this journey. The act of helping each other can be a powerful tool although it's not essential to this process. If you already have someone you want to share this with, that's great and it can be very helpful. I'll go into more detail on this collaboration process a little later in the book.

One of the main things I want you to recognize is that you can create whatever you want to have in your life. You are the artist. You're the one holding the brush to the canvas. You hold the "master key" to all your future success. By using this book, and by understanding and working on the principles and techniques contained in it, you will be able to accomplish whatever it is that you wish to accomplish. I am your guide, and together we will help you fulfill your dreams.

I will also be talking about some of the universal laws that govern our lives. Whether we choose to take heed and believe in them is a personal matter, but our lives are, in many ways, ruled by them, so I think it is best to use them to our advantage. Of a different species but similarly relevant is the Law of Attraction which states "like attracts like," so the more you fill your life with positive people and things, the more positivity will be attracted to you. As we delve into some of these laws you will learn how to benefit from the forces that exist in the universe and apply them to your life.

Throughout the book, I ask you to do some exercises. This is important, and I encourage you to take those exercises seriously. They will all come together at the end of the book to help you create your future. Change is an inescapable constant, so the question is, "Are *you* going to be in charge of the change?"

With that in mind, we'll begin looking at the specifics you must learn. This is how you go about creating the future you've always dreamed about.

Today will never happen again.

Don't waste it with a false start or no start at all.

Og Mandino

ONE

WHO'S IN CHARGE ANYWAY?

I'm going to start this book by telling you something that might be difficult to hear, and by doing this, I'm aware that I'm running a risk. I'm running a risk that you might decide not to read this book at all. You might put it down right now. But if you do that, you will miss out on an abundance of opportunities ahead of you, so I encourage you to continue. Once you understand the simplicity of what I'm about to tell you, you'll understand how easy it is to change not only your future, but your life, and your financial situation. Are you ready?

Have you ever thought about who's really in charge? I mean, who is your real boss? I'm not talking about the boss at work or the boss at home – at home it might be your spouse, it might be you, or it might even be your kids or someone else. But really, ultimately, the boss is you.

You are the one who has the ability to create whatever it is you want in your life. Now I'm going to take that a step further: in fact, *you* are a product of all of your past decisions. You are where you are at today because of every decision you have made. That's true in all aspects of your life, not just in business. You are what you are today due to the choices and decisions you've made in the past.

Before you read on, stop and pause for thirty seconds and think about that. You are the product of all your decisions. Think about some of the decisions you have made that brought you to where you are today.

If that's true, now think about this: what can you do to change things from now on? To make sure your future is better and brighter? What decisions can you make to change your future? We will be looking into that!

CHAPTER ONE EXERCISE

Before you can change your future, you need to take stock of where you are at and what is going on in your life today. This exercise should give you the motivation you need to move from your current situation to a new reality. Think about things carefully for a while and **write down** the answers to these questions.

- If you could wave a magic wand to make your life easier, what is the first thing that comes to mind? What is the number one thing that would improve the quality of your life? Was your first thought lots of money? We often link these two things in our minds, so let's break it down a little. These next discoveries may be a little painful, but they are necessary.

- What would help you to have a long life? Your health is obviously a major consideration here; if you are fortunate enough to be healthy currently, this may not be a concern for you yet. But imagine if you were to lose your health; what would happen then? Would you be able to continue living in the house you're in? Who would pay the bills if you couldn't work for a length of time?

- Do you get to spend enough time with your spouse or partner, your children, and your friends? What would enable you to spend more time with them? What do you feel you're missing out on by not having enough time with them?

- Do you look at other people around you and wonder why their lives always seems to be easier than yours and go to according to plan? Does it seem like others always get what they want, when they want it? Are you jealous of someone who seems to go on vacation whenever he or she wants and who always seems to have a new car?

- If you could choose one place in the world to go on vacation, where would it be? It might be somewhere you've visited before and loved, or it could be a dream destination you've always wanted to visit. If it's the latter, why have you not been there yet?

- Would being a "millionaire" be enough? And what does being a millionaire mean to you? We'll get into this in more detail later.

Now that you have answered these questions, continue to contemplate them and add to your answers as you read further through this chapter.

Chances are that the answers to most of these questions relate to your finances, or lack thereof. So what can you do, right now, to change all this? You're here and you're reading this book, so you must already have some desire for change. What if the pressure to keep at your current job was removed? Imagine having the freedom to choose whether or not to work today. What would that give you? How much would that enrich your life and the lives of those around you? How would you feel about being able to go to the park or the beach whenever you want? How good would it feel to take your spouse out for a romantic meal without worrying about paying the bill?

I'm not saying everything is going to be easy. I'm telling you here and now that you will face some challenges, and there is "work" involved. But what if you could work *smarter*, not just harder? Doesn't that sound like an attractive prospect? What if you could put a system in place that would allow you to live the kind of life you currently envy?

Now I'd like you to flip that around and imagine yourself six months, a year or five from now if you *don't* take the action steps that follow. Close your eyes and really think about it – *feel* it. You will still be worrying about paying the bills, still be watching the pennies. You'll be choosing restaurants that are *good*, sure, but not *great*. Will you still be driving the same car, worrying about the fact that it needs new tires, and fearing the mechanic? What about the kids' school vacations? Will you be staying at home and trying to make the best of it? What kind of birthday gift will you be able to get for your partner?

Your results will vary depending on the action you take now. If you're still reading, perhaps you're ready to take a leap into the future. Sure, it's an unknown entity at the moment, but doesn't that make it rather exciting? Imagine all the new opportunities that will open up for you when you take a decisive step into a new beginning. You've held back up to now for one reason or another, but no more! Now is the time. Now is *your* time.

Your current and future decisions can change everything in your life, from your financial situation to your personal relationships with family and friends, as well as your relationships with business associates. The decisions you make today and in the future can actually change everything about your life. The fact that you're reading this book tells me that something has changed. You want your future to be different from today, and you want to start working on it right now.

Your future is an extremely exciting prospect. As you learn and complete the steps in this book, you're going to realize just how exciting it can be. Sure, you may read a few things you've seen before, but my method will allow you to understand them, grasp them differently, and implement them. I'm going to help you to organize these ideas and strategies in such a way that you'll be able to take action and succeed. The steps are very simple. They're very straightforward, yet they can seem deceptive to people who don't know how to use them effectively, or who don't comprehend the magic that can happen in the brain. This book is a step-by-step guide that will take you where you want to go. It functions as a roadmap of exactly how to get there.

Understand that it won't be enough just to read and study your way to success; it doesn't work that way. Success requires action, not complacency. The ideas and concepts contained in this book are going to require action on your part, and action is the only thing that will suffice. Studying and reading alone aren't going to cut it here.

Since the economic collapse of 2008, the world is different. Everything has changed, and what you need to do in order to get ahead has also changed. It is critical that you take charge of your life. No one else is going to do it for you! Don't expect your company, your union, or your government to look out for your future; it simply won't happen. If you truly want to make a difference in your life, and in the lives of those you care about around you, then you must take charge. Now is the time to make some decisions if you want to get ahead. Believe me, you can do this. We are here for such a short time, and the way to make a great life for yourself is to take action. You're going to put in the hours and the work anyway, so why not grasp some new opportunities along the way? Why not be the best you can be? It *is* possible.

Money is going to have a greater influence in your life than virtually any other commodity you can think of. It is important for you to understand this. Believe me, I've lived it. Going through bankruptcy was devastating. As I said in the introduction, I had very little money at the time. At one stage I had no income at all. Simply paying rent and putting food on the table was no easy task, but I did it and I eventually managed to get back on top, thanks to the techniques in this book. I turned misfortune into a fortune, and so can you, by setting goals and taking action. Goals without action are only dreams. It's not that dreams are not worthwhile – in fact it's quite the opposite. As you will see, they are a beginning step. But our dreams require the foundation of action in order to become our realities.

All of the physical manifestations around us started with a thought or a dream. But you need to understand that millionaires aren't simply dreamers: they're people who take action. They conceive of great concepts, and then they take action to manifest them in reality. I know it sounds easy "for someone else." And, it's all too easy to get too comfortable with your current position and not worry about trying to get ahead. If that's really what you want, then you're probably not interested in reading this book, although I sincerely wish you the best. But if you're not happy with the status quo, read on.

Recall: you are the product of all your decisions. You are also a product of what your subconscious mind has created. The problem is that you have probably not been directing what your subconscious is working on and creating for you. We'll talk much more about the subconscious and how this works later in the book, but what's most important right now is that you understand that you can have whatever it is that you really want. No matter what you conceive, you really can manifest it. Each step along the way is a step toward creating exactly what you desire for your life.

My advice at this stage is to surround yourself with people who are 100 percent supportive. Involve only those who want to come along with you on your exciting new journey. For now, keep your new dreams and aspirations to yourself, away from those who are already negative or unsupportive in your life. When some people hear about someone who wants to create something better in his or her life, their minds are conflicted because they don't understand. They can't figure out how you're going to get there. What they *do* understand is that they may get left behind. The conflict they feel may create a negative manifestation of their feelings toward you, and they could potentially create a roadblock for you. It's easy for these people to have comments or opinions, but as Napoleon Hill says in *Think and Grow Rich*, "Opinions are the cheapest commodities on earth."

There are going to be people in your life who choose to stay behind. Maybe it's because they're not prepared to take on the same kinds of challenges that you are. Potentially, they're going to live hand-to-mouth and day-to-day and life may always be a struggle for them. They could change their lives too; however, they may not be prepared to do what is necessary – to do what you're about to do. And that's where you are different. You've seen negativity, and you're ready to take positive action. That's what's going to set you apart from the crowd. You're ready to re-make your life.

As we move forward and you start to understand some of the concepts laid out here, you may feel confronted by them. My ideas and ways of doing things may challenge some of the concepts that you currently hold dear. How quickly do you want to move from your current position to a new level of success in your life, a new level of freedom? Because it can be done in a relatively short period of time: small steps at first, bigger steps in a little while, and then leaps and bounds as you discover the power you have over your own life. The question is this: Do you really have what it takes? Do you have a burning desire and the ability to commit? Are you capable of absolute, dogged persistence?

Albert Einstein said, "Information is not knowledge." You're going to come away with some information. It will then be up to you to take this information and turn it into useful knowledge for yourself by putting it into action. Through action, you'll begin to internalize the material, and it will become actual knowledge for you. It will become knowledge so inherent and so deep-rooted within your psyche that you will be able to create anything that you desire.

We've all heard the old saying, "Give a man a fish, and he'll eat for a day. Teach a man to fish, and he'll eat for a lifetime." This book *teaches*. There's a lot of information out there on becoming successful but what we are doing here is filtering and focusing some of what is "out there." But more importantly, we are putting it into usable simple action steps that actually help you to create whatever it is that you want. These initial action steps are the exercises in the book; there are nine in total. You have already encountered the first one earlier. Not difficult, but important. Each exercise builds on the previous one, concluding with your ultimate actions and the Master Key, which will truly program yourself to the successes you desire using your seven-minute PPM. And when you do this, you will find that the tasks required to achieve your success are much more enjoyable and you will most likely look forward to them each day with enthusiasm.

As we start to move through the book, it's important that you don't fall into the "analysis–paralysis trap" because again, what is important, is action. Action is the only way to create your new life.

It's essential to take time to gather the information you need so that you will be able to turn it into useful knowledge, and you will need some time to analyze that information, but action is what's going to be the key. You have the opportunity to change your life, starting today. As you read this book, you'll find places to practice the techniques with some exercises that will hopefully prove the simplicity of this strategy. These exercises will also expose areas of your life you may need to change or do some work in.

Some people, even those who choose to read this book, simply won't make the changes that are required to significantly alter their life for the better. They will make excuses or have "situations" come up. They let life get in the way. I sure hope this won't be you. I do not want you to let life get in the way. Don't let your job get in the way. Don't let friends get in the way of your personal achievements and happiness. Don't let the television, or YouTube, or Facebook get in the way of you creating the life that you want. You can do it, and it is worth it! There are many, many time-wasters out there. It's important that you analyze how you're spending your time each day so that you can maximize your ability to accomplish everything you need to accomplish.

The Bank of Montreal in Canada did a survey, and 34 percent of the respondents said they were counting on a lottery win to fund their retirements.[1] That's over a third of the people who answered – that's a huge problem. Do not be one of those people. Your chances of winning the lottery are infinitesimal. In fact, I'm sure these statistics are the same throughout the world, so don't count on the lottery.

What's it going to take for you to make the decision to change your life? Some people need to hit rock bottom before they make a move. If you're already at rock bottom, then now is the time to understand you don't have to stay there. If you're not at the bottom, why go all the way down? So many people today are alive physically, but mentally they're dead. They don't think of the future, and they're so tied up with living day-to-day, or even living in the past, that they are unable to move forward. It's a sad fact about society today. But if people know they have the ability to move out of the muck they're in, then they begin to look forward and change their lives in ways that will truly set them free. In fact, by using the techniques in this book, we can create an atmosphere throughout the country – even throughout the world! – that's extremely positive and uplifting for everyone.

Now it's time to do something different and start preparing yourself for success. It doesn't take much. It doesn't take long. In fact, it only takes about seven minutes (hence the title *The Seven-Minute Millionaire*). We're going to delve deeper, and I'll give you all the details you need to see how seven minutes is going to change your life.

You can do this. You already have everything it takes to get everything that you want.

The world today has so many different avenues in which you can create your success. Think of all the companies that were started in garages and college dormitories: Google, Facebook, Twitter, and so on. So many companies have started from nothing; a few years ago they were merely ideas, and now they're worth billions. That may not be your area of expertise, or anything like what you want to do, but whatever your dream is, you can get there. Whether you want to be the best realtor you can be, the best lawyer, the best net-worker, the best father, the best spouse, the following techniques will help you get there. All I'm asking is that you take a bold step forward. You must take a chance. Bet on yourself and the chance you'll be successful. All you are risking is your own improvement.

HOW HIGH DO YOU WANT TO GO?

The next question to consider is what level of success do you want? There's no downside to taking charge of your life and implementing these techniques right now. Unless you do, you will remain on your current path. You'll stay in a place that you don't want to be. Remember, nobody can take charge for you. You must do it yourself. You alone are responsible for putting in the time. Remember when I said it was just seven minutes? Those seven minutes are going to make all the difference in the world. Simply remember and understand that you're the boss. You're in charge of you. I like to call it "You Inc." Just think of yourself as a business. If you *are* the business, then who's in charge? *You are in charge of you.* Sure, you probably have a boss at work, but that's not what we're talking about here. When it comes to *your* choices, *you* are the boss.

One of the typical stumbling blocks for people who are trying to set and reach their goals is the ability to *follow through* with a commitment. One reason is that it's easy to get side-tracked. It's also easier to stay on your current path and let the status quo shape your life. There is no question that persistence is one of the key elements in attaining any sort of success. The techniques in this book, combined with your seven-minute PPM, will enhance your ability to follow through and gain the persistence that you may have lacked in the past. You will find that your mindset is quickly changing about the best methods to attain success. Not only will you find it easier to stick to all of your commitments and goals, but you will also realize that procrastination gets you nowhere. If this is not an issue for you now, you will find your success comes even more quickly.

It's also important for you to remain open to the program. You must be willing to be *coachable* and *teachable*, and if you are a type A personality, this may not come naturally. However, allow yourself to be coached so you can achieve what you desire. Understand what it means to take a little direction. Have some faith in somebody who has been there and done it. Learn how to use these proven techniques; they can help you to get out of the muck you may be in at the moment. I keep alluding to techniques, and maybe the whole thing is sounding a little esoteric so far, but, let me tell you something you probably don't realize: you're already using the techniques I'm talking about. You may not have understood their significance yet, and you may not be using them to your advantage. You might be letting your environment control your future. We are going to change that significantly.

At the moment, you may not be programming your subconscious mind in a way that allows you to move forward. Knowing *how* to program, manipulate, or mould your subconscious mind will allow you to attract everything that you desire. When you learn how to program this, it will become absolutely clear that you can attain whatever it is you're after. What I'm talking about is life changing, and I've used these exact techniques on myself to earn millions of dollars.

One thing you do need to understand is that these techniques are *not* going to prevent you from having setbacks along the way. In fact, even utilizing these techniques, I still have, situations and opportunities that pass me by. I have made some mistakes that cost me large sums of money – in some cases, *millions of dollars* – but I can't, and won't, dwell on those. Instead I made sure I learned from each situation. We all need to keep moving forward; there is no reward in looking back. If I were to dwell on a current mistake rather than using it as a learning opportunity, a way of fine-tuning myself, then I would be missing out. Those who dwell on mistakes may not have the ability to achieve what they're looking for. I make conscious decisions to move on, as you must; that's the only way to progress in this world. Living in the past does nothing for those of us who aren't historians!

I've traded currencies for a living. When you look at a currency chart, you can see significant moves in one or more currencies on a regular basis, daily. Some of the changes are so significant that if you were to risk large enough amounts of money, you could make tens of thousands or even hundreds of thousands of dollars or more in a single day! But the unfortunate thing about the currencies market is that you can't predict the future with absolute certainty, and even if you are right about the direction, you can't be sure about the timing. The fact is when you look at the opportunities missed, they are moments that you can never get back. There is little point in thinking about what you *should have* done.

This is not meant as a lesson on the many facets of currency trading, but the point is that if I focused on missed chances rather than looking for current opportunities and those in the future, I would either not be able to trade at all, or I would lose all my money chasing situations that have already happened. It's important that we learn from the past, but it's more important that we all look to the future. It's extremely important that you decide, right now, that's what you're going to do. You can move forward; I can help.

No decision to act is without other considerations. You must make a conscious decision that you're going to move ahead and that we're going to work together throughout the pages of this book. You can set yourself on a course toward a better future, the future that you're truly after.

Don't worry at this moment about how we're going to accomplish this, or how to get it right. Now is the time to make a decision to make a difference in your life. It's time to start moving forward. The old saying, "Insanity is continuing to do what you've done before but expecting different results," has been attributed to Benjamin Franklin, Albert Einstein, and others, and is a commonly understood principle. It's time to make a change. As you go through the pages of this book, don't simply seek just external motivation. I want you to become inspired. I want something to spark inside you. Because when that fire ignites from within, when you are inspired, then you become unstoppable.

By the end of this book you will be unstoppable! This is my goal for you.

When you do what you fear most,

then you can do anything.

Stephen Richards

TWO

REALLY, WHAT IS IT YOU WANT?

D o you really want to be rich? I mean, do you actually want to be a millionaire, or even a billionaire? These are important questions, and I don't ask them flippantly. Many people don't recognize what they could really do with that kind of money; they almost fear having too much money. Before we really get into that, we're going to take care of some of those boring housekeeping things in this chapter – you know, the things we all find a chore, like paying the bills and putting food on the table. Don't underestimate the importance of these tasks, however, as they represent the first thoughtful steps in this entire process. These chores anchor us and our future, while playing an important part of our foundation for success.

First, I want you to ask yourself what success really means to you. Have you given this a great deal of thought? Remember the exercise in chapter one? Have you actually pictured what success looks like to you? Because when I ask "What does success mean to you?" I'm also asking, "How much money do you want to have?" The amount of money you want will determine some of the action steps you're going to take. Yes, we're going to talk about more than just money, but bear with me for a moment while we focus on this very important aspect of your life.

When I was going through my bankruptcy, I was so short of money that I could barely feed myself, and money was, of course, a real focus in my life. What I realized then is that *where you are* today is not *who you are*. Although you may be a very good person with great intentions, you might not have any money. Money does not define the person within. You may have the ability to achieve greatness, but you're just not there *yet*. That's where I come in.

There is a marvelous synergy when you go from wishing for something to actually making it happen with focus and purpose. There's great joy and a great deal of fun to be had in accomplishing great things. What you can accomplish is amazing, but it's also important to recognize that greatness can be achieved by making fractional changes. Tiny alterations to your life will make a profound difference. We could be talking about thousands of dollars, hundreds of thousands, or even millions of dollars, all by making just a few minor changes in the way you go through your life.

Does chance or luck play a part in your fortunes? Michael J. Mauboussin, head of Global Financial Strategies at Credit Suisse Bank, had the following to say about the stock market when he spoke with Tim Bowler of the BBC's *Business Daily* program: "Luck has become more important in defining outcomes today than it was a generation or two ago. When we see bad outcomes, we tend to associate those with a lack of skill."[2] However, he did point out that it's important to recognize that both skill and luck can make relative contributions in the world of business and investing. It's a funny thing, though – I find the harder I work, the luckier I get.

While something like roulette comes down to pure luck, other activities, like chess, rely on your skills, but the outcome is affected by another person's actions. A game like poker requires a combination of luck and skill. You see the same people at the final table of many of the tournaments, but no matter how they follow the rules and play the odds, it comes down to the hands they're dealt and how they play with the other people at the table. Have you relied thus far on luck or skill, or a combination of both? "Knowing where you are on that continuum allows you to think much more effectively," Mauboussin continued in his BBC interview. There are two different scales for you to distinguish between: relative skills, "mine versus yours," and how good you are absolutely. As you go through the book you will find there is very little real competition for you to worry about.

To get ahead in life, you must be able to balance risk and reward, and understand that without any risk, there is either very little reward, or it may be of limited value. I'm not asking you to risk your house or car here, but merely to understand that you need to put something out there in order to gain greater rewards. This could mean an investment of time, rather than cold, hard, cash, although cash outlay does have its place. And generally speaking, starting any business takes some money, even if it's just a few hundred dollars.

Over the past few decades there has been an explosive growth of readily available information, resulting in a narrowing of our relative skills range (the difference between the very best and the average). So how do you become the very best, rather than simply being average? Average is no longer good enough for what you desire in your life.

Professor Richard Wiseman of Hertfordshire University in the UK says, "It's about embracing uncertainty."[3] Warren Buffett once famously commented that risk "comes from not knowing what you're doing." But if you follow the seven-minute program, you will not only know *what* you're doing, you'll also be planning *when* you want to do it. Half the excitement of a journey comes in the planning and anticipation of it. We're about to use the process outlined in this book to plan and create your future – this will be one of the greatest journeys of your life! There is a part within your brain that neuro-scientists call the interpreter; it tends to associate a good outcome with good skill. So once you begin to understand your strengths, you can capitalize on your assets even further. Before we can get to that, you need to take a look at where things are here and now. Do you know what your net worth is? It's important that you know.

CHAPTER TWO EXERCISE

You did the first part of this exercise in the last chapter when I asked you to list the things that were part of your idea of "a better and brighter future."

- Expand on those ideas now by writing down every-thing that you want to buy or do with the money you're going to make. Be specific and list, one by one, the things you would definitely buy or do as part of your better future. Think of things like what restaurants you'd choose, the cost of the wines you'd like to drink, or the expensive stores you've avoided but at which you'd like to shop. Include even the simplest things that a wealthy person might almost take for granted.

- At the same time we also need to form a true picture of where you are today. If you don't know where you are at the moment, it's going to be difficult to see your progress.

44

- Calculate your net worth, being very specific. Be sure to list all of your assets and the things you currently own. Then calculate what these items would be worth in monetary terms if you were to sell them today. How much do you think you could you get for them?

- Next, take a look at all of your liabilities. How much money do you owe? Do you owe money on your car? Do you owe money on your home? Do you owe money on credit cards? Take note of all the debts you have, including any money you owe to friends and family, and then add them all together.

- Now subtract your liabilities from your assets. I hope that at the end you're left with a positive number – the bigger, the better! That's your net worth. If your number is negative, then okay, that's the reality for now and you'll deal with it.

Now you are on your way to the better, brighter future you were thinking about in chapter one. Of course, if you're not ready for change yet or you're still a little frightened by the prospect of change, then I urge you to reread what you wrote about how your life would be in six months if you were to remain stagnant. You've already begun the preliminary ground work you need to do before you can begin utilizing the techniques we are beginning to utilize and learn, as we move forward through this book. This foundation is important so be sure to take it seriously.

I realize the exercises where I ask you to expand on your previous list and be specific about what you'd like to buy are more fun than the exercise determining your net worth, but both are important. Your net worth is what you will receive ongoing income from and retire on, assuming you decide to retire at some point. The higher your net worth, the more you'll be able to actually enjoy your retirement. Ideally, retirement will be a special time in your life, representative of a new beginning rather than an ending.

It's a sad fact that many people need to reduce their lifestyles in order to retire. Many financial advisors actually expect their clients to do so. I can't understand this school of thought. Personally, I am the opposite: I would like to *increase* my lifestyle if I retire. I want to enjoy my life even more than I do now by travelling more, enjoying the world more, and seeing more of my country. I know these things cost money, and if I don't have the net worth to be able to do those things at that time, then that will be an issue for me. That's why it's important to discover where we are today and figure out where we want to be, financially, in the future. Once you know your net worth, you may have a few more ideas about what you would like to do with your money. For example, have you always dreamed of retiring somewhere where the weather is warm and the pace of life is slow? Now's the time to start making plans to ensure that your dreams can happen in reality.

Daydreams are pleasant pastimes, sure enough, but reality can be so much more exciting and fulfilling, especially when you know that you've earned it. All this and more can be achieved when you use your daydreams "on purpose" to develop and engage your own seven-minute Personal Programming Message (hereinafter referred to as PPM). The power of the PPM will become clear later in the book, but it is the key to achieving your dreams.

TIME IS MONEY

Let's focus again on having money and what that means to you. But before we get there, let me ask you this: Are you prepared to change the way you use your time? Are you willing to stop watching television, or at least cut down? Are you prepared to unsubscribe from the useless emails that you receive on a daily basis? These are examples of time wasters: things that take up valuable time that would be better spent elsewhere.

I'm constantly unsubscribing from email lists that I somehow get onto. Sometimes they may be good and informative, but I have to discriminate because I know my time is extremely valuable. *Your time is extremely valuable too.* Often I will unsubscribe from emails that may be perfectly good – or cute, or funny, or otherwise entertaining – because I really don't have time for those at the moment. If you wish, you can set up your email to filter the funny ones into a separate folder. Then when you have downtime – and you will want downtime – you can go back and view them. Just don't allow them to penetrate the time when you're actually working and trying to get ahead. That's the time that you're "in action," busy making a better life for yourself. Interrupting that time is a sure-fire way to slow your progress and sidetrack yourself. You don't want to picture a future that matches the past, do you?

From now on, most of your time must be spent *doing* rather than *observing. Taking action* rather than *reacting.* Take control of the elements in your life that require a reaction, and determine whether it is a *time-wasting* reaction or a *productive* action.

BE NOT AFRAID

Have you ever thought about the greatest challenge facing people when they're trying to change their lives, make big decisions, or simply get ahead? For most people, the greatest challenge is fear. Think of the word FEAR as an acronym for **F**alse **E**vidence **A**ppearing **R**eal. People also worry – to the point of inaction – about what might happen. Fear is very similar to worry in that way. Some of us fear failure and some fear success.

There are many unknown things you might fear about your upcoming success. For example, what if your wealth changes the dynamics of your friendships? Old friends may not be able to afford to do the things you want to do, and you may find that they don't want to hang out anymore. These are real fears, but I don't want you to worry. You can always make new friends along the way, friends who share similar outlooks and you can also maintain the old friendships if you feel you'd like to. As your life changes for the better, you will find that the kind of people you mix with will naturally change. You will be mixing with other successful people!

So getting back to that money, how much will it take to obtain those things on your list? What else are you going to do with it? How much do you really need? Think about your needs and your desires, because they're two different things. The question then becomes, truly, how much do you desire? Because "needs" can often be fulfilled with a welfare check. But desires, they're different, and that's where the burning inspiration must come from. Go back now and look over the list you made earlier. By now your list probably comprises of almost everything and anything at all that you've thought would be good to have in your future.

Many people's lists will include buying things like great cars. Maybe you picture yourself with a Ferrari or a Lamborghini. Or maybe it's a boat you want. Maybe you've added things like being able to order great wine at a restaurant or building a wine cellar so you can enjoy great wine at home. Maybe you'd like to have steak once a week instead of once a month, or you'd like to be able to hire a vegetarian cook to come and cook you delicious, specialized vegetarian meals you've never even heard of!

Think about the home that you would like. How big would it be? Would you stay in the neighborhood you're in now? What about home automation? Would you have a spectacular media room? Maybe you want to build a completely eco-friendly home, that will cost a great deal of money. Later on we'll talk more about getting actual physical pictures of these vehicles, these "things" that you want in your life, these desires that you have, and what you're going to do with them.

What really does it for me is great wine. I know a little about wine, not enough, but I'm constantly increasing my knowledge. I also love to drink great wine, and I make sure to take care of it and store it properly at the correct temperature and humidity. Wine may not be something that interests you in the least-your "bag" may be specialized sports equipment or vintage whiskey-I'm talking about the material things money can buy. We'll talk more about the other aspects of your life in a while, but it is important for you to carry on updating that list as new items you'd like come into your mind. As we go through the process of this book, of the topics we cover might give you further ideas or inspiration as you continue to add to your list.

The strategies within this book are going to help you attain your goals and dreams more quickly if utilized than if not. But this is not a short term experiment or "quick fix." I want to ensure that you're rich for the long term. Just remember that if something appears too good to be true, then it generally is. What you want is sustainability and longevity. You may have tried, as I have in the past, the quick fix when you've been desperate, but you already know that doesn't work, or you wouldn't be here now. If you're young, maybe in your 20s, and reading this book for the first time and all of these concepts are new, well you're really in luck because this is an amazing opportunity for you to guarantee your wealth. In *The Richest Man in Babylon*, George Samuel Clason says, "Pay yourself first. Pay yourself 10 percent of everything that you bring in. It's important that you don't spend everything you make. It's important, in fact critical, that you learn to save. By paying yourself first, this makes you rich automatically."

THE PENNY PRINCIPLE

Let me show you something now. I'm going to make you two virtual offers. I'll give you one cent right now, and then I'll double it and give you double that amount each and every day for an entire month. Or, I'll give you one million dollars right now.

Which offer would you take? If you were the person who said, "I'll take the million dollars please," you may be surprised to learn that if you started with one penny today, by the end of the month you would have $10,737,418.00 rather than the one million dollars that you took. This is the power of leveraging. Have a look at the chart below:

TABLE 1. Results of Leveraging One Cent Over a Thirty-Day Period

Day 1	$0.01	Day 2	$0.02
Day 3	$0.04	Day 4	$0.08
Day 5	$0.16	Day 6	$0.32
Day 7	$0.64	Day 8	$1.28
Day 9	$2.56	Day 10	$5.12
Day 11	$10.24	Day 12	$20.48
Day 13	$40.96	Day 14	$81.92
Day 15	$163.84	Day 16	$327.68
Day 17	$655.36	Day 18	$1,310.72
Day 19	$2,621.44	Day 20	$5,242.88
Day 21	$10,485.76	Day 22	$20,971.52
Day 23	$41,943.04	Day 24	$83,886.08
Day 25	$167,772.16	Day 26	$335,544.32
Day 27	$671,088.64	Day 28	$1,342,177.28
Day 29	$2,684,354.56	Day 30	$5,368,709.12
Day 31		$10,737,418.24	

On day 14, you're only up to $81.92. On day 20, you're only up to $5,200. Even at day 25, you're only at $167,000. But the power of leveraging really kicks in around day twenty-five. By day thirty, you've got over $5,000,000. Archimedes, the Greek mathematician once said, "Give me a big enough lever, a place to stand and I could move the world."

THE POWER OF THE COMPOUND PRINCIPLE

You may have heard that if you were to start putting money away in your twenties or thirties, you would be able to retire as a millionaire. It's absolutely true and you don't really need to be in your 20s to achieve this. Take a look at the tables below that show us how compounding works. You'll see something similar to the penny principle above; the powerful effect of compounding doesn't kick in right away.

This first table is simple. It shows the effect that different interest rates will have on the same initial investment. Although you may not have $10,000 to invest right now, that isn't the point of this table. Instead, observe how a compounded return can exponentially magnify the end result. Just look at the difference after twenty-five years at 5 percent versus 10 percent versus 20 percent. And then look what happens when you add five more years of compounding, the difference is staggering.

TABLE 2. The Effect of Different Interest Rates on One Initial Investment of $10,000

# Years	5%	6%	10%	11%	15%	20%
5	$12,834	$13,489	$16,453	$17,289	$21,072	$26,960
10	$16,470	$18,194	$27,070	$29,892	$44,402	$72,683
15	$21,137	$24,541	$44,539	$51,680	$93,563	$195,950
20	$27,126	$33,102	$73,281	$89,350	$197,155	$528,275
25	$34,813	$44,650	$120,569	$154,479	$415,441	$1,424,214
30	$44,677	$60,226	$198,374	$267,081	$875,410	$3,839,640
35	$57,377	$81,236	$326,387	$461,761	$1,844,648	$10,351,554
40	$73,584	$109,574	$537,007	$798,345	$3,887,007	$27,907,480

*Figures in all tables are rounded up or down to the nearest $.

** Interest in all tables is compounded monthly.

Tables 3 and 4, included in Appendix B, show how the variables of compounding can really affect the outcome, one with an initial investment of $1,000 and a continued deposit of $200 per month and another table with an initial deposit of $100 with a $100 per month deposit. It is really quite amazing. Be sure to have a look.

You're the one

creating your life

and your future.

As you can see, the effects of compound interest are really quite amazing. If you're in your 20s you should absolutely start putting some money away each and every month: 10 percent of everything you receive. In fact your savings account should be the first expense off of your paycheck each and every month. If possible, create an auto-debit system that takes money from your paycheck and puts it directly into a savings and investment account.

Yes, we have to find ways to get returns that are greater than the simple interest rates the bank gives you, but that's a subject for another book. One thing is for sure: you must become competent at talking about money, and you must try to understand the basics of investing. No one, and I do mean no one, has a greater vested interest in your money than you. Even financial advisors with the best of intentions will have certain personal or corporate biases that might conflict with your personal objectives. It is best to seek financial advice from independent sources whose incomes are not derived from selling any stock or investment. These advisors should make their money by providing excellent advice. There are excellent independent advisory services you can use, which I also use, to invest and receive greater returns than the local stock exchange and/or bank. But beware of bad services

I hope this table and the ones in the Appendix demonstrate the value of compound interest. I know I started the table at 5 percent, and today's banks only offer a fraction of that. But as I said, it is important to find ways to beat the bank and stock market. It is doable, but it will take some effort. It really is amazing how the numbers work over a period of time. If you're in your twenties or thirties now, don't delay! Start today and open some form of investment or savings account where you can grow your money, preferably tax-free, over the next however many years until your retirement. In the words of Albert Einstein, "Compound interest is the eighth wonder of the world. He who understands it, earns it, he who doesn't, pays it." When you start to save money, opportunities will arise.

If you're already in your forties, fifties, sixties or older, you may not have as much time to allow for the compounding effects of a small monthly investment. To achieve the wealth you seek, you will need to either deposit larger sums of money each month, or take greater risks with your money. All risks must be taken carefully and with a great deal of consideration of your own personal circumstances. I have made millions speculating on "penny stocks" and know others who have done the same. But these risks are not for most people, and certainly not with all of your money. Building a business is another kind of risk, but at least you have more control over what happens than you do if you own a piece of a company on the stock market.

You can play with the numbers yourself to calculate how much money you would end up with over different periods of time. There are many simple online calculators. I like the one at the following URL because it lets me adjust the variables to my own liking: http://www.thecalculatorsite.com/finance/calculators/compoundinterestcalculator.php.

An easy way of summarizing what I have just said is to reiterate: if you're young, start today. Save as much as you can, but make sure that's a minimum of 10 percent of your paycheck and any other money you receive. You'll automatically make yourself rich. Even if you're older, you should still save. Start putting aside money for your retirement, for getting ahead, for building wealth. When you have it, you will be able to take advantage of the opportunities that come your way.

To become wealthy and really get ahead, you must do whatever it takes to get your personal finances in order as quickly as possible. Don't go into debt. Pay off your credit cards every month. These are extremely important principles that I live by, yet I also understand that when there's more month than money, it can be a difficult thing to do. But it is important that you not be the one paying the interest.

If you are already in debt and having trouble with it, find a way to consolidate it. This means paying off all of your high interest rate debts with another loan at a lower interest rate so you are making one affordable monthly payment. Talk with your creditors to see if they will allow you to pay off your debt with no interest or at a reduced interest rate. Sometimes a creditor will be happy to receive the principal because if you declare bankruptcy, they get nothing. If you do this, also ask if they will let you pay only the principal and none of the compounded interest you have probably accrued. There are services that can help you, but be sure they are legitimate and not just taking a fee from you and doing nothing.

You may need to find a way to increase your income, either through a second job or maybe by creating a part-time small business from your home. Maybe your small business will eventually grow and earn you a lot of money like mine did. Don't risk a lot to start; if you can, choose something with low start-up costs, but with the ability to earn enough money to cover your living expenses every month. This will give you an opportunity to get ahead. Even then, remember to pay yourself first.

As I said, it's extremely important for you to have a basic understanding of money and finances. You don't want to be taken advantage of by someone telling you they're smarter than you when, in fact, they may just have a little more knowledge on a particular topic than you currently do. Knowledge is power.

Starting a business is the realm of the entrepreneur, and a start-up business may be your best way to get ahead. You want a business that's going to get the cash flowing in quickly. Later, we'll talk about how to make your brain flow with new ideas on a regular basis, but don't worry too much at this stage; there are many, many opportunities, and the right one will occur at the right time.

The concepts I'm talking about now will, as you employ them, free you from the shackles that currently hold you back. One of the very interesting things about having money is that it seems to make you more like the person you actually are. People often use the phrase "money corrupts." While this may be true for some people, money only has the power to corrupt those who are corruptible. You've probably also heard that "money is the root of all evil." But the actual quote from the Bible, Timothy 6:10, is "the *love of money* is the root of all evil . . ." Even while you can appreciate the difference that money will make to your life, it is also important to remember that you will still be you, with the same values and morals. If you're already a nice person, money is just going to allow you to be an even nicer one. And while it may be true that money doesn't buy happiness, it does make life a lot easier.

Now we have some of these housekeeping ideas out of the way, in the next chapter I'll talk about some of the concepts behind developing your money-making strategies. It's important that you understand the concepts before we get into developing the strategies for your success, so that's where we'll begin.

If something is not impossible,

there must be a way to do it.

Sir Nicholas Winton

THREE

EXPECT IT AND IT WILL COME

In the last chapter, we talked about money and having money. We talked about what you would do with the money. In fact, I asked you to write down some of the things, no matter how crazy they might be, that you would like do with that money. As you do each of the exercises you will begin to see how each one builds upon the last. The process itself will help you understand and believe that what you are doing will allow you to create the life you are after because you will define the specifics of what you are after. But this isn't just goal setting, this technique goes far beyond that. Maybe you're not ready to believe just yet, but have a little faith in this process: if you follow through with what I'm talking about, you will accomplish what you set out to achieve. I wonder what you're expecting when you read that. Are you expecting a positive result from this? Is there a little devil on your shoulder saying, "No, no, no, don't expect that. I can't believe that"? Your expectations, whether positive or negative, can have a dramatic effect on what it is that you actually accomplish. These expectations are not just about money, they're about every aspect of your life.

I'd like you to think about what kind of things you expect to happen on a daily basis. Do you generally expect things to turn out well, or do you expect them to turn out badly? When you go into a parking lot, do you expect to find a spot right near the place you're going, or do you expect the lot to be full? When I drive into a busy parking lot, I fully expect to find a spot exactly where I want it, and very, very often, I do. There are definitely occasions when I don't, but most often, I really do find that perfect spot.

I expect positive things to happen to me on a regular basis. I expect the best of people in general and generally that's what I get. Am I ever disappointed? Sure, that happens, but that's reality. However, using your PPM and this process you will find that your life follows what you are setting your sights on. How you deal with disappointment can make a difference to your direction and to the outcomes you attain. In this chapter, I talk with you about putting yourself in a position where you'll be able to acquire the things you're after. We'll begin to align your expectations in such a way that you will start to expect everything in your life to happen in the way that you want it to. I understand that may not be where you are today, and that's okay, but don't worry about that for now. We'll get there. I don't want you to worry about losing or having money. As you continue with the steps in this book, you are going to get to that point – to the point where you barely even consider the things that worry you currently. I don't even want you to worry about how you will achieve your goals and create the money and freedom you are after. As you create your PPM, your accomplishments will become easier and more enjoyable. To quote Bob Marley, "Don't worry about a thing/ 'Cause every little thing gonna be alright." In fact, I don't even like using the word "worry" because I don't want to give it any power in your life.

We're now getting into the more interesting and compelling information of the book, where you will begin making decisions that will attract money to you through your conscious decisions, and subconscious programming. This will help manifest your conscious expectations.

Your own expectations can be a blessing or a curse, really, because if you're expecting negative all the time, you may find that you get it. In *Be Careful What You Wish For*, Alexandra Potter says, "Consider the implications. We think we know what we want, but we can never really know until we've got it. And sometimes when we have, we discover we never really wanted it in the first place – but then it's too late."[4] So when I tell you to be clear and positive in your expectations and later in your seven-minute PPM, make sure that you are; your future depends on it. This is no time to be wishy-washy; you need to be definite. Make sure you want it! Creating your PPM will help you to receive what you desire in all areas of your life.

Because many of the expectations we have in life actually manifest themselves in the real world, clarifying and creating your expectations is part of the process as well. You can actually program yourself so that the expectations you have are positive ones, and so that the fulfilment of these expectations will also be positive and what you actually want.

When you take a close look at people who are successful in their chosen fields, you will see that they mainly mix with people who are similar to them and who hold similar beliefs. To look at that on the flip side, imagine the down-and-out alcoholic who lives on the streets. He will be mixing with people who know where to go to get out of the cold for the night, and he will also be with those who know where to get alcohol. Is he likely to change his mind-set by mixing with the people who show him where to get more alcohol? Possibly not. He will continue living his life as he does. Conversely, the successful businessperson will always have an eye for the next opportunity and will go out of their way to make it happen. That's not to say that the businessperson would not help someone less fortunate than themselves, but they also understand that you have to want things to change, in order to make those changes happen.

When you expect something good to come into your life and you work toward that, then it will happen. It happened for me and it will happen for you; just open yourself to the many possibilities. Everyone is good at something. Now is your time to shine. And when you set your PPM in motion, you'll be amazed at how this really works!

You can choose to improve at expecting more in your life, or you can choose to have lower expectations. Lowering your expectations is fine, as long as you're prepared to live with what those expectations bring. We're on this earth for a very short period of time, and I think we might as well make the best of it. So I like to expect great things and produce great things. Here's one of my personal expectations: I've been taking vitamins for most of my life in an effort to stay healthy and live longer. I also work out as often as I can, and because of these factors, I expect to live to be 125 years old! That may sound crazy to you; who even wants to be 125 years old? My expectation is not just to exist to 125; I actually expect to live a healthy 125 years and enjoy every single one of them all along the way. I've carried this expectation for a very, very long time, and it's become a part of what I believe. Will it happen? I don't know, but that is my expectation.

As you specifically plan your success, you're going to build an expectation of it. You'll be able to change your mindset once and for all, and once you understand these simple principles – what I call "the master keys to success" – and how to correctly apply them, then you'll be in a position to create what you desire at any time throughout the rest of your life. Taking the small amount of time now to develop and learn these skills is absolutely critical.

I have a sailboat and, occasionally I like to set the autopilot to take us where we're going. I am the one responsible for setting the course, and I have an expectation of how we're going to get there. However, the winds and the tide battle to take us off course on a regular basis, so the tiller and helm constantly shift and change, putting us back on the correct course. To expand on that a little, over time we're probably off course for most of the trip, but with the adjustments made along the way, we ultimately end up at our programmed, desired destination.

So, as much as we plan for the future, we also need to be able to adjust along the way to get back on course. We're going to set our sights on where we're going, our ultimate and intermediate goals, and along the way, we're going to adjust as needed to get there. Some people might say, "Oh, you got lucky. You just got there," but it will be a conscious effort. Conscious decisions and thoughts, and preconceived ideas will get you to where you are going. For me, expectations are more subconscious than conscious, and the subconscious mind is far more powerful than the conscious mind. Still, it is the conscious mind where we conceive our pathways in life.

As I mentioned earlier, these techniques can be employed in areas in your life other than financial security, such as relationships and weight loss. Some people take the scenic route meaning they are really not directing their life, they are floating along and allowing outside influences to direct them. Some people take the highway, meaning they are in control directing exactly where they are going, how they are getting there and therefore getting where they are headed much more quickly. The end results may be the same – assuming you get to your chosen destination – but the timing and route taken may be different.

You may expect you are going to get where you desire to go, but then life gets in the way. Maybe an event like a birthday party or a wedding celebration comes up. What you do next is the important thing: Do you allow the event to throw you completely off course? Or do you take it as a small diversion and remain focused on the planned course you have set and get back on it as soon as is possible and practical? Your conscious decisions will determine whether you are on the scenic route or on the highway to success. The adjustments you make along the way can make all the difference to your chosen journey. Your PPM will keep you on track at all times, but especially during times of distraction.

You might argue that the conscious mind, where we make decisions and dream up ideas, is more important than the subconscious or vice versa since the subconscious is also our body's control center and controls things like our breathing and the pumping of our heart. However, the two work differently and together; that's the beauty of these techniques.[5] You have the ability through your conscious mind to change what your subconscious mind is targeting and moving you toward; through programming, you can use it to change your expectations. Doing this also changes the conscious mind and brings the two into alignment. People will often refer to this lack of alignment as limiting beliefs, which they are. Your PPM allows you to reprogram your beliefs and overwrite them, just as you would overwrite an old computer program with an upgraded version. This may all sound like a game, but believe me, it's not. It really does work, and it's important that you expect prosperity and picture what you really want. Think big and shoot for the stars; if you only get as far as the moon, that's still not so bad. Having said that, this book is teaching you how to reach those stars.

As I previously mentioned, don't let yourself be influenced too much by other people. In fact, start to think about the people around you and what they expect. Do they expect to get ahead themselves? Do they expect *you* to get ahead? The people around you who have great expectations also have the ability to influence you, but it's best to not allow this unless their expectations for you are positive or they are working with you in your mastermind group.

Think about children in school. Many parents set certain expectations for their children, for example, they're going to college, and that's just the way it is. That's one kind of expectation, and it is often one that is fulfilled. In other families, the expectation is, well, nobody else went to university, so nobody has to go to university. That kind of expectation is also often fulfilled. Perhaps a family has a generational history of being on welfare, and they never do anything to escape that reality. Expectation can begin at a very young age, so if you have children, consider helping them to expect great things from an early age, just like my mother did with me and my two brothers. My mother always said that we could do whatever we wanted to do, and when I told her at the age of ten that I was going to be rich, she fully supported me. "That's great," she said. "You can do that, for sure." Within no time I had my own paper route; I was responsible for purchasing the papers and collecting the money from the subscribers each month. I quickly built myself a lucrative little business. I was constantly looking at business ideas and ways to start a business. I sold plant seeds and greeting cards door-to-door. I was determined, even at that early age that my expectation of becoming rich would come to fruition.

That expectation was not only in my head, but also reinforced positively by my mother. If she had responded differently when I made my declaration and said something like, "Oh no, no, you could never be that successful," then maybe my idea would have been beaten down and it would not have happened.

At one point, I worked at a bank and had been in a clerical position for almost a year. I had decided that was no longer the direction I wanted to go, and I gave my notice to quit. The manager came to me and said, "Okay, but we've decided to put you through the management training program." In hindsight, this was a really excellent offer, but at that time I was very young and didn't fully realize the opportunity before me and I chose to refuse the offer. But when I turned him down, the bank manager said, "You know what, if you don't take this offer, you'll never amount to anything." Fortunately, he was wrong and I don't regret my decision. My expectations were so very strong and so very set, that even at that stage his words just rolled off of my back. I can admit that I did have a moment of doubt when he said that, but I thought, "No, I *have* to do this. I'm moving on."

All the decisions we make have the power to change our lives one way or the other, sometimes positively, sometimes negatively. My bankruptcy and my decision to leave the bank changed my life positively. It's up to us to create our own success and choose the direction we want to go. You can do this easily. It's important that you're aware of the possibilities, and you will begin to generate ideas and possibilities for yourself as we go through some of the additional exercises. For the moment, ask yourself if you have a specific direction in mind. What do you wish to attain in order to create the life that you want, to create the wealth that you're after, to create the freedom that you're after, and to create the relationships you long for?

Do you have these things firmly in your mind right now? Do you know specifically in which direction you're going? Maybe you don't, and that's OK. If your objective is to start your own business, maybe you need to start going to franchise shows, start looking online for different business opportunities, start reading success magazines and online magazines with success stories. Discover for yourself what other people are doing to create success these days. There are so many opportunities available in the world of franchising and other industries! Ask yourself what you're good at and what you enjoy. There are ideas online all over the place. One way I made several millions was in the business of network marketing with a company selling a weight loss product and nutritional supplements. I was open to listening and capitalized on the opportunity.

CHAPTER THREE, EXERCISE ONE

In the last chapter you wrote down things you want to "have" or do with the money you make. Now I want you to write down random ideas of things you would like to do in the future. You have done some of this in the previous list, but now as you become aware of the possibilities, you'll become aware of even more possibilities.

This is true in all areas of life, and not just business. One opportunity will lead to another, which leads to another and then another.

Feel free to add to your list of places you want to go and the list of other things you wanted to do. But are there things you would like to do that may not be about the money you will make? For example, do you want to volunteer for a charity or start a business? Do you know what kind?

The things you might want to do will in fact be the things that take you where you want to go. It's important that we keep ourselves open to ideas. If somebody asks if you're interested in something, it's often best just to say yes and hear what they have to say. Unless you listen and digest the information, you never know where it could lead. It may turn out that you're not interested in the specific situation they're talking about, but maybe this person will be the one who leads you toward someone who can help you. Maybe the new person can help you to get where you're going.

With more experience you'll learn to make judgments about what is right for you more quickly. Even the multi-millionaires of Shark Tank and Dragon's Den look closely at seemingly crazy ideas brought to them by entrepreneurs before saying no. Take a page from their book; look and listen first.

CHAPTER THREE, EXERCISE TWO

As I mentioned previously, each exercise builds upon the last and you will be using what you have created to develop your specific seven-minute PPM that can and likely will change your life. Just now, though, your exercise is to write down all of the different things you would do if you could live with no constraints. They can be ideas that you want to accomplish throughout the rest of your life, not just those you would like today. In fact, what I'm really talking about is creating a "bucket list." Although I don't personally like that term, we'll use it here because I think it's become an idea most people understand. You are expanding further on what you have done already and some of what you have written down may be part of this list.

- Write down everything you'd like to do before you die. We'll refine this later, but for now simply brainstorm and write down everything that you can think of for your bucket list.

- Think about what you want out of life? Include things like relationships: what kind of relationship would you like in your life? What kind of charitable or spiritual work might you do? What do you want in all aspects of your life?

Do this list as though your life depends on it because your life actually does depend on it. Expecting abundance is a key factor in how you're going to achieve it, and having this list opens the mind to those expectations. As we get closer to creating your PPM, I will ask you to be more decisive. You'll pick and choose some specifics to focus on both now and in the future. We'll be dealing with both long- and short-term objectives, so we'll look at your goals for seven years from now, five years, one year, monthly-to-month and so on.

If we don't know what we want, then how are we going to get it? It's like my sailing story: if I were to just sit and let the helm lead the way unpiloted, then the boat would constantly go in circles or get caught in the wind and tide. I'd either go nowhere or end up on the rocks. But when I set the autopilot, or steer toward a point on an island across the water, I know exactly where I'm going, even if there are several course corrections to be made. Similarly, you need to know, clearly, what your objective is and what you're shooting for. This is the start of quantifying, clarifying, and then monetizing exactly what it is that you're after.

These lists form the early stage, but it's important you make your lists because complacency kills. If you just sit back and think, "Oh, I don't need to do this or write anything down. I'll read the next chapter because that's what I want to do right now," then I'd ask you to reconsider. Take out a pen and paper or get on your computer, and begin making your list *right now*! If you were to spend twenty or thirty minutes on this, I'd bet you could come up with a hundred different ideas about what you would like.

Don't limit yourself at this point. Just start writing, and let your brain tell you what you'd like. If you get stuck, then get up and walk around for thirty seconds, come back, and see if you can write down another ten or twenty ideas. Only then should you carry on reading the next chapter because it's all about being aware and avoiding this complacency. Take charge right now. No more procrastination and the next chapter will be a piece of cake for you.

As you build your list of possibilities, you can begin to expect them, but if you haven't decided what you're after, how will you know what to expect?

A real decision is measured by

the fact that you've taken a new action.

If there's no action,

you haven't truly decided.

Tony Robbins

FOUR

ACTION SPEAKS VOLUMES

I n the last chapter, we talked about expectations and how important they are for creating your dream life. I hope you had fun writing down everything you want to accomplish in your life and contemplating the many, many things that you want to set out and do over the coming months and years. When you look at that list, do you find it daunting, or does it excite you? Do you believe that it's going to happen? Do you *expect* that it's going to happen? I certainly hope you do, but at this point it doesn't matter too much because your PPM will help instill that confidence into your subconscious and conscious mind.

As I said at the end of the last chapter, complacency can have a very detrimental effect on your success. If you don't take action, then nothing will happen, and that is all you can expect. Keep in mind the ideas you've already come up with, and keep adding to the list as new ideas spring into your mind. These ideas are valid because they are your ideas. As Napoleon Hill said in *Think & Grow Rich*, "What the mind can conceive and believe, it can achieve."

Recall I mentioned the Law of Attraction in the introduction: like attracting like. The more you open up to new ideas, the more ideas will naturally come into your mind. It's almost a "snowball" effect. You are training your brain to be an idea producer. This is one of the reasons I have asked you to do the list exercises, and even though there is some overlap in them, they are valuable for training yourself to have a constant flow of ideas. Another idea creator is to challenge yourself to read articles about topics that are new to you. When you take in new knowledge on interesting topics, be they medical, technical, or any other topic, new ideas can naturally occur. Choose something well written that interests you. Become an idea generator!

Getting back to inaction and complacency, they are probably the biggest barriers to your success right now. Procrastination will limit you for the rest of your life. As the proverb says, "Tomorrow never comes." Today is the day you must take action. Worrying about things is just counterproductive, and it takes too much positive energy away from you. Worry limits your expectations, and most of what you worry about will never happen.

Understand that *action will overcome worry and doubt*. When you take positive action, many things in your life will begin to change, and people around you will notice. They will start to see that *you're going places*. Actions do speak louder than words. As soon you put your plan into motion, it gains momentum. Newton's first law of physics states that an object in motion tends to remain in motion. Once you start the ball rolling, the more momentum it gathers, the more likely it is to continue. Your positive motion becomes hard to stop or interrupt. You'll find that opportunities like you've never had before will open for you, and the whole process will be extremely energizing. The plans and the actions you take will quickly build upon each other, giving you more energy, like the boost you get from working out.

Daily, I want you to choose the things that are going to help you become a happy and successful person. That's the beauty of this part of the exercise: you get to choose what you do. Even if you have to go to a boring job every day, you choose how you deal with that job. You can choose to make that job more fun today than it was yesterday. In fact, I suggest that you begin today by doing more at work than what you're actually paid to do. Establish a good attitude about this, and eventually, whether at that job or in another situation, you will be paid for more than what you do.

That's really the truth about how you want to live your life. Do more than what is expected, and in the future it will come back to you in a very big way. People often fail to achieve some of their dreams, but it's not necessarily from a lack of action, but a lack of *effective* action. They take action, or think they're taking action, but that action may not actually be moving them toward their objectives.

Every day, I would like you to ask yourself the following questions: Was what I did today effective? Did it move me toward my objectives? If it did, then great! Continue along those lines. But if it didn't, stop and think, and recognize why. Think about changing or correcting something in your actions to make them more effective. Don't wait for tomorrow. You will often hear people say, "The timing isn't quite right yet. It's not perfect." That's not acceptable. You can't wait for everything to be "perfect" or "just right." You need to take action now.

Things are never going to be perfect. Indeed, avoidance is the thief of time, so the right time is now. Your life needs a plan of action because if you don't know where you are going, you might just end up somewhere else. You should also take care of where you live – your environment – as well as your body. Yes, that's what I said: take care of your environment and your body.

It's important that you eat well and maintain a good level of fitness. If you're not currently exercising, get yourself in shape! Walk or bike places instead of driving. Take the stairs instead of the elevator. Simple, small changes to your behavior and habits can reap huge rewards on your state of mind, your physical health and well-being.

Nutrition is extremely important when it comes to our ability to make decisions; eating well increases mental energy as well as physical. Try and cut out all the foods that are of no benefit to your body or your brain, even if they are delicious. Eating well increases your immunity, and your general health and well-being, and it can affect your ability to concentrate. Additionally, by cutting out the fast-food joints and other rubbish, you will also be saving money, which will help you to pay the bills. Fast food doesn't come cheap, neither to your wallet nor to your health.

Here is a quick guide to foods that are not only considered to be "brain food," but are also good for general health.[6] Watch for them, and try to plan your meals primarily from these as often as you can.

- WHOLEGRAIN FOODS. Nothing works properly without a good source of energy. Whole grains aid our abilities to concentrate and focus by providing a steady stream of glucose in the flow of blood to the brain. Choose slow-release whole grains, which will provide energy all day long, keeping the brain in top form. A breakfast of oatmeal is an excellent way to start your day.

- OILY FISH. Essential fatty acids, good for extra brain boost, are called that for one reason: they are *essential* and cannot be made by the body. Therefore they have to be obtained through diet. The most effective occur in oily fish, such as salmon, pilchards, mackerel, trout, sardines, herring, and kippers.

- TOMATOES. Yes, the humble tomato is a wonderful thing. Tinned or cooked tomatoes are said to be even better for you than fresh ones, so be sure to add them to most savory dishes. They are a rich source of lycopene, which is a powerful antioxidant that helps to fight against dementia and other similar conditions.

- NUTS AND SEEDS. If you are tempted to snack on chips, swap them for nuts and seeds, in particular, pumpkin seeds. Keep it to a small handful, though, as the oils in nuts are very high in calories. It is best to eat these raw, not cooked in oil and salted.

- DARK GREEN LEAFY VEGETABLES. Add these to most meals for an added boost of vitamins and minerals. Vegetables like kale, cabbage, cauliflower, and broccoli are extremely good for you and have several anti-cancer ingredients in them.

If you have health issues, don't say, "I'm going to get in shape once I retire or have money." You really need to get in shape now; it's important. Don't wait. If you have money without health, then what good is the money? You can't buy great health. You need to be in shape so you can enjoy a long, healthy life and appreciate the fruits of your labor. I usually go to the gym three to five days a week, taking the weekends off. I do a combination of spinning (riding a stationary bike), core exercises, and some weight training. I strongly recommend you put in place some form of an exercise program.

Yoga and palates are very beneficial. Spinning is great cardio exercise, great for calorie burning, getting in physical shape, and losing weight, if that's what you're after.

I also strongly suggest that you start some form of strength training if you don't already do so. It's important to keep your muscles dense to help regulate your metabolism, which in turn assists in keeping your weight down. Muscles burn fat very efficiently and the denser the muscle tissue is, the more efficiently they burn fat. After age forty, we lose nearly 8 percent of muscle mass per decade, and that loss accelerates as we age. It's very important, therefore, to build and maintain muscle mass through some form of resistance or weight training exercise.

I used to suffer from a great deal of back pain; at times, it was so incapacitating that when my son was about two years old, I couldn't always lift him off the floor. This was really upsetting to me, so I went to the doctor. I had an MRI scan, I had a CAT scan, I went to the rheumatologist, and they injected me with radioactive isotopes to look at my bones through an X-ray. I had everything checked and they couldn't find a thing. Not a thing!

It felt like an extremely severe case of sciatica with severe shooting pain down my leg, and it would occasionally switch from the left to the right, more often settling on the right side. I couldn't figure it out and it wouldn't go away. At that time in my life, I wasn't really exercising much. I was in fairly good shape, or so I thought, but I wasn't really on an exercise plan. Then I got a personal trainer who introduced me to core exercises. Core exercises may be one of the best things you can do for yourself, in addition to some sort of cardio. They strengthen all the muscles through the middle of the body that keep you structurally sound. The core muscles are like the foundation for your spine. Just as you need a good solid foundation on a house or a building, you also need a strong foundation within your body – your core.

I understand if you can't afford to go to a gym right now – don't forget, I've been there. But there are so many exercises you can do at home. Yes, I know it takes discipline, but it can be done if you are determined to get things right. Look online for core exercises, or look up strength or body weight exercises that you can do anywhere. "Planks" are quite simple really, and have become something of an internet phenomenon. They involve holding your body straight, like a plank, level to the ground, and they don't require any equipment. It's amazing how this one action will strengthen the muscles in your back, abdomen, and core. You can increase the intensity by lifting a leg and lifting an arm. You can do lunges, which are simply stepping forward into a deep knee bend. You can also do them to the side. You can always get a ball and do roll-ins. Roll-ins are done by placing your hands on the floor and then putting your shins, tops of your feet or toes on an inflated ball and then pulling or rolling the ball in toward your shoulders. You can also do them on your back by placing your shoulders on the ground and your heals on the ball. But many exercises don't require any equipment whatsoever. OK, my disclaimer is that you should start slowly so you don't injure yourself and always consult your doctor before you start any rigorous exercise routine.

So now there is no financial excuse. You don't have the money to join a gym, but you can still get fit. It may seem that I'm going on about this more than you think is necessary in a book like this, but it is so important to be healthy. You will find that a good healthy body and a good healthy mind work together synergistically. By working for a healthy body, you will automatically improve your mind's health as well.

Maybe your excuse is that you don't have the time. In that case, look at ways you can make more time in your current day. Every extra little bit of time that you manage to find, no matter how small, can have a profound impact on your health, as long as you use that time wisely.

We've talked about cutting out things like television, but have you done it yet? That's not to say you can't have some downtime, but maybe you need to set specific times that you'll watch your favorite show (or two or three!); or use a digital video recorder so you can control your schedule. There is some good quality television out there; you just need to be selective with your viewing.

Reorganize your time so that you're moving toward your objectives and doing the things you want to do on a daily basis. Always keep your goals in mind, and make sure you're heading forward toward them.

Do you drive for around an hour or more per day? Instead of listening to music, think about what you need and want to learn, and consider listening to recordings that take you toward your learning goals. If you listen for just an hour a day, you'll find about 350 hours per year available for learning new things. Even if you were to drop the weekends, you would still find up to 250 hours a year to listen and learn. That's a lot of learning! You could probably learn an entire language in that amount of time.

Another language might help you if your new business is an international one, but there are many, many things you can learn. Find recordings online and download them onto your iPod or phone. Plug them into the car. Or take CDs or DVDs out of the library. Library cards are free! There's loads of easily available information out there for you to learn from, if you take advantage of it.

How much time do you spend sleeping every night? Could you get up earlier? Could you train yourself to get up earlier? Do you really need eight hours of sleep, or might seven be enough? Could six be enough? I know some people who only sleep for four or five hours.

For me, four or five hours is not enough sleep. I can get by and work well with six. When I was already selling real estate full-time, an opportunity arose to start my own business, which I took. I was on the west coast, and in order to deal with people in the east (a three-hour time difference!) I decided that I would get up an hour early. I made myself get up at five in the morning, when it was 8:00 a.m. back east, and I would begin making calls at that time. I gave myself an extra hour a day, but this hour allowed me to build a multimillion dollar business!

Would you ever have thought that a person could create that much additional wealth simply by having an hour less sleep? If you thought it was that easy, you would have already tried it, wouldn't you? Sleep is important and necessary to repair the body and the mind, but it may surprise you to discover you need less of it than you thought.

You can find ways to make more time for yourself, no matter how full you think your week already is. I often hear excuses from people: "Oh, I'm too old." Oh, I'm too busy." "I have too much work to do." "I have the kids to look after." There are a variety of excuses, some of which are valid, some of them less so, and some of them not valid at all. Look carefully at how you spend your time – and I mean every minute of it – and you will find *somewhere* you can create some additional time. Maybe you need to drop unnecessary habits or pastimes that do not serve you. If you have people in your life who are a drain on your time and your mental and physical energy, then you need to either drastically reduce the amount of time that you spend with them or drop them entirely.

The truth is, it doesn't matter to anybody else or the universe at large whether you become successful or not. If you allow situations and excuses to get in the way of your progress, then you're allowing someone or something else to steal your dream. Are you prepared to let that happen? I know you're not: that's why you're reading this book!

I'd like you to think about the things in your life that are working against you right now, the things stopping you from getting where you want to go. What is the biggest roadblock? Is it something or someone? Is it one element or is it two? Or maybe there are several things that are getting in your way. It's important first to recognize what's getting in your way. Until you identify what it is, it's very difficult to eliminate it. Once you've pinpointed the issues, you need to plan how you can eliminate the distractions, or roadblocks, that are currently in your way.

Maybe you can't eliminate them completely. Maybe you have to figure out workarounds, ways to detour around the issues so you can
still get to where you want to go. Sometimes when I'm sailing, I find a
log in the middle of the open water, and I need to sail around it to get
where I'm going. You must find a way to do the same thing in daily life.

It's just as important to plan your day and plan your time because
it's so easy to waste time. I learned a valuable lesson from one of
the top trainers at the time when I was in real estate, Tom Hopkins.
One of his key messages was to "Do the most productive thing at
any given moment." Think about that for a moment. Considered
another way, "Is this the highest and best use of my time right
now? Are these actions going to get me where I want to go?"

It's easy to sit at your desk and shuffle papers or do the easy things
that you must do on a daily basis, but those aren't the things that
are really going to get you ahead. Is it really important that the gar-
bage be taken out right now or can it wait for an hour until you have
downtime? It's so easy to let little things get in the way of achieving what we set out to accomplish, but I encourage you to have the
discipline to not let that happen. As you move forward with your
plans, and you create your PPM, you'll find that you have an increasing ability to discipline yourself. Right now, however, I want you to
understand that no matter where you are in your life today, you can
change your situation. You can become financially free and have all
that you desire. Remember, *where* you are today is not *who* you are.

Each of the exercises is designed to help you grow a vision of your
future and a vision of who you want to become. As you grow the
picture of the person you want to be and get familiar with where

you want to be in life, it's also important that you start to become that person. Act like the person you want to be, making it a bit of a game for yourself. Start by thinking about who you want to be in the future, and instead of leaving it until "the future," be that person today. Step into that person's shoes and feel what it's like to be the person you want to be. Close your eyes for a moment, and visualize the clothes you would be wearing if you had the finances to shop wherever you'd like to shop. *See* how good you look, knowing that the moment you have been waiting for is not too far away.

Looking to, envisioning, and creating your future is the point of each of the exercises I have given you. We don't want to spend our lives looking back except to learn from the past, or to recount and enjoy a wonderful memory. Always look forward. Looking back and focusing on the past can and will stop your success.

As I have said, I give my mother a great deal of credit for encouraging me to think and to become the person I am today. She was the one who instilled the belief in me that I am capable of doing whatever I want to do. However, as she has aged, she has developed a tendency to look back. She's now considering all of the things in her life that she thinks she did wrong, and she focuses on these moments in her past. They cause her great distress; however, she is working on getting back on track and I am hopeful for her future.

You can choose not to do what I'm suggesting, but if you continue to look backwards, you will find that you actually start *going* backwards. Backwards and downhill.

The only way to create and build your future is to look forward.

Reflecting on the past and learning from it is important, but dwelling on the past and agonizing over it will do you no good whatsoever. We're actually going to take this a step further. You're going to "pre-live" the future. Pre-live and actually rehearse the events or actions or accomplishments in your head before you get there. This is what's going to help you to get there and achieve your goals.

You may have heard the story Jim Carrey told on the Oprah Winfrey show in 1997. Before he became famous for *Dumb and Dumber*, he struggled for a long time with a lack of finances and emotional support. No one believed in him. When he was out of work, he spent many hours in libraries, learning about psychology and business and the power of visualization, and pre-living a future event. He dreamed of earning $10 million for a single acting role, and he wrote himself a check for that amount. He would look at it and touch and feel it, closing his eyes and dreaming of a time when he would really be able to bank such a check. He post-dated it for a time in the future, Thanksgiving 1995. Just before that date, he found out he was going to make ten million dollars for *Dumb & Dumber*. He told Oprah that when his father died, he put that check in his father's casket because it was a dream they shared together. This is how powerful visualization can be.

You've probably also heard stories about Tiger Woods and other golfers, Formula 1 race car drivers and, in fact, great athletes of all types. They are renowned for visualizing the course in their mind before they play it or drive it in reality. They'll play each shot and turn each corner. They'll focus on it, they'll picture it, and they'll understand it. Tiger Woods will picture the stroke he's going to make, how the ball comes off his club, how it spins in the air. He'll follow the flight of the ball in his mind, picture the exact spot where he wants to land it, and then watch it roll where he wants it to go, creating a picture in his mind. This type of focus, this type of *pre-living* is key to being able to achieve those results in reality.

You cannot force the results that you want. Determination and persistence are absolutely critical, but determination alone will not manifest your desired results. You must cultivate them in your mind first, and don't confuse this action with persistence. Although persistence is also key, it's a different element. Building your future in your conscious mind will allow your subconscious move you toward it.

We've already talked about not living in the past. *Most* people spend *most* of their time living in the present, spending most of their time on current results, and living day to day – almost hand-to-mouth. Of course we need to live in the now and be present in everything we do, enjoying each experience and moment, but to move forward along a new path, we must also forge that path in our minds, and look to the future in order to create it.

The truth is that there is no standing still. You're either moving forward or backward, so focusing on today's results only, without any forward thought or creation in your mind, is almost like moving backward. The world is always moving forward and time is advancing, so unless you're advancing with it, you are, in fact, being forced backward. Every second that passes by without our taking action to create our future becomes the past, and if we let this persist, we become passengers in our own lives instead of the captains.

CHAPTER FOUR EXERCISE

In this exercise we are going to find out how effectively we are using our time and how much time we are actually wasting.

- For the next seven days write down everything you do throughout the day with the time noted beside each action. If you have a day planner or something similar, write it in there. Track your actions in five minute segments, so you can go back and analyze exactly how much time you spent productively. If you don't have a planner, you can use a journal or a something like a Google calendar, which is available free with a free Gmail account.

- Analyze precisely how much time you spent doing what: downtime, personal maintenance (showering, shaving, etc.), working out, driving to work, working, and so on.

- Once you have done that, go back and calculate your productive time and your unproductive time for each of the seven days.

- Break your times down into your productivity at work and at home and working toward your goals and enhancing your relationships by spending time with your partner or family. These are really the three main categories of time we have. Most productive things will fall under one of these headings.

- Look very closely at your unproductive time. What

were you doing? Because if you weren't working or working toward your goals, what is it you were doing?

It takes some inner strength to be able to do this exercise honestly, but it's really important that you do an honest evaluation of yourself. There's no point in trying to fool anyone at this stage; you'll only be fooling yourself. If you take this exercise seriously, it will help you to move forward toward the next point and the next set of exercises, all of which will soon come together in your seven-minute PPM. Remember, procrastination can be a dream killer. There's no time like today because tomorrow never comes. Tracking your time will provide you with a clear picture of how effectively you are using your time today and allow you to make changes that can free up the time you may need to begin to build your future.

I hope you come away from this chapter feeling energized, feeling positive, and thinking about all of the things that you can accomplish now. Hopefully you are also starting to think about ways to find more time within your normal day to accomplish more toward the future you want. You should also have a clearer idea of time you're currently not spending working toward your goals.

In the next chapter, we're going to talk about positive thinking and the significance of it. We'll also address the fact that positive thinking alone doesn't make you successful.

Go as far as you can see.

When you get there,

you'll be able to see farther.

Zig Ziglar

FIVE

BE A VISIONARY

In chapter four we talked about the importance of taking action and not procrastinating. Never underestimate the power of getting started today. I know it's easy to put things off until tomorrow, but when we do, the success that we can have is seriously challenged. No one ever got anywhere in life by practicing procrastination, and deservedly so. We also talked about using a portion of our unproductive time constructively to learn and grow, and how those choices can yield significant improvements for us down the road. And we introduced the concept of picturing the "future you" in the future you want.

Those of us who are considered to be "lucky" actually generate our own good fortune through our thoughts and behavior. As I said earlier, the harder I work, the luckier I get. "Lucky" people:

- Create and notice the chances for new opportunities.
- Make "lucky" decisions based on intuition.
- Have positive expectations that create self-fulfilling prophesies.
- Bounce back with a resilient attitude when things don't work out as expected.

"Lucky" people possess a very proactive kind of attitude; they are apt to think "let's get out there and do it," whereas those who consider themselves to be unlucky tend to say, "I'm not going to do it because there isn't enough payback." Rather than being analytical, those who are "lucky" grab every opportunity that comes their way, realizing that life can be uncertain and full of chances that are there to be seized. Those who think they're unlucky are shown in personality tests to be more anxious than others who seem to be lucky in life. This anxiety causes tension, which can interfere with the ability to notice the unexpected possibilities that come their way.

Sometimes it's good to embrace uncertainty. An experiment was carried out by Professor Wiseman where he asked a group of volunteers to focus on a dot in the middle of their computer screen. For the first test group, now and again other dots would appear, flashing on the edges of the screen. Virtually everyone in that group saw these flashing dots. Another test group was told there would be a large payoff if they continued watching the dot in the center of the screen. The possibility of a payoff created some anxiety, and more than one third of the second group didn't notice the other flashing dots.[7] So what can we learn from this? The fact is that the harder you concentrate on something, the less likely you are to see other opportunities. That goes for your business life as well as your personal one. That said, once you have set your course, it will likely require a great deal of focus on your part. But I think you can see what I am saying here: there is a difference between being blinded by unrelenting focus and being focused on a task or goal.

Your mood is also extremely important in increasing your luck. When you're in a great mood and feeling relaxed, you will discover that your mind becomes more expansive. You have to learn to embrace uncertainty and to have the flexibility to say "Hold on, things could be different." You therefore also need to learn to be less rigid in your attitude. Just because you've always thought things go a certain way doesn't mean that's true. We now live in a world full of technology, where things can change radically in a short space of time. Perhaps one of the keys to increasing your "luck" is allowing yourself to create your own chances.

If you believe that luck is a ruling factor in a person's destiny, then chances are that you are superstitious in other ways as well. What role does superstition play in how lucky you are? Maybe you carry a rabbit's foot, four-leaf clover, or some other talisman around with you. Does it mean that you're wasting your time? Having a talisman symbolizes our attempts to impose some kind of order on our universe, and as such we would assume that these efforts are doomed to fail. However, Cologne University carried out a series of experiments that would suggest there may be a role for superstition after all.[8] In one of these tests, researchers handed out golf balls, telling the recipients, all of whom played golf, that they were "lucky" balls. In other tests, golfers were allowed to carry their own superstitious charms. Interestingly, in both of these experiments the players who carried their own charms or lucky balls performed better than those who did not.

The fact that they were holding superstitious charms seemed to boost the golfers' confidence in their own abilities. As a result, they enjoyed an enhanced performance. My conclusion then, is that if a charm or talisman seems to work for you, then there is no harm in continuing to carry it. This is besides my belief that what you put into life is what you will ultimately get out of it. I don't have a lucky charm, but if that works for you, that's OK.

So what does luck have to do with a book on creating your future? Am I saying that you have to be lucky to achieve success? No, not at all. I am simply making the point that feeling "lucky" can have a positive influence on the subconscious mind. To me these results are not only interesting, but they prove that your beliefs can influence your results. Our beliefs are largely held in our conscious mind, but we can change our beliefs, without a lucky charm, using the programming techniques and your PPM.

In this chapter you're going to learn how you can make positive changes that will physically manifest themselves in your life. You will also learn how you can start realizing the goals you've already set, or are about to set, for yourself. You've probably read books on positive thinking before this one, or maybe you've heard speakers talk in front of a room about the importance of positive thinking. We all know how crucial it is to set a positive mental attitude for yourself. While this is certainly important and can lead to some good in your life, I want you to realize something important: positive thinking, in and of itself, will not make you successful.

As we discussed in the previous chapter, unless you take action, nothing significant will happen, and your life will continue as it has up to now. The fact that you have made it this far into this book proves that you want more than that. You want better for you and your family, and therefore you're going to take action. Right?

I've got friends and acquaintances who go through their days and their lives *thinking* positively, *talking* positively, *and appearing* to be extremely positive people. However, they've never been able to manifest any success in their life. Why is that? It's because they haven't been taking quality action. They haven't utilized their subconscious minds to take action on the goals they have set for themselves. What is it that sets people apart? What is the difference between those who think positively and those who both think positively and are able to take the appropriate action? I think there's another element here that we've talked about already. We've covered the importance of visualization. We've talked about how Tiger Woods will picture his shots and play an entire round of golf in his mind before he steps onto the course, but *what else does he do*? Surely he doesn't simply picture it in his mind, go and play, and that's it.

What else does he do? He practices and he practices and he practices . . . and then he practices some more! Like any professional, Tiger and others like him practice before they act in the real world. They don't put themselves at risk without preparation. I don't mean putting yourself at physical risk here, but it could be emotional or financial.

Humans face many types of risk in their lives, but in most cases, that risk is simply fear. Remember: **F**alse **E**vidence **A**ppearing **R**eal. And as previously mentioned, most of what we fear never comes to pass. OK, I have another exercise for you. It's simple and quick.

CHAPTER FIVE EXERCISE

I would like you to visualize a tomato, a simple tomato. I know you've seen a tomato many times before, so you can decide if it's red or green, on or off the plant. You can decide if it has a few leaves or none. Picture that tomato in your mind. Maybe it's hanging on the bush or maybe it's on its own. Maybe it's in a bowl along with other tomatoes. There's nothing special about that is there? But wait . . .

Can you smell that tomato? Can you see if it's a perfect tomato, or are there a few little blotches on it? Now I'd like you to visualize the slicing of that tomato. It can be you or someone else slicing it, picture that tomato being sliced. Picture some of the juices starting to flow from it, ending up on the cutting board or counter.

There is a reason behind this simple exercise: I wanted you to take something simple and picture it because I think everybody can do that. And if you can visualize a tomato, even a little bit, then **you can visualize and create your life**.

This is because the *vision* of what you're going to create *precedes* its creation, and it precedes the action that you must take to get there. The exercises that you've done to this point are exactly that: exercise. They are precursors to formalizing your visualization plan and creating the seven-minute PPM that can change your life. So this visualization of a simple tomato is a very important step in helping you to understand the process we're going to use.

Don't be afraid if you had a little difficulty visualizing the tomato to begin with. As you practice you'll get better, just like Tiger Woods. He still practices to this day so that he can get better, and it's the same for every other professional person out there: as they practice, they get better. With the techniques we're going to formulate over the rest of this book, you'll find that your fear will dissipate and you'll start to move through the process with greater and greater ease. If you let fear take charge of you, then you'll find it has the power to be self-sabotaging. This is no good for anyone!

If you start to believe the fears you have are real, you might go into a "state of no-decision," the state of paralysis or procrastination, which is, in effect, self-sabotage. Oftentimes, we have a fear of failure or even a fear of success, as we discussed earlier. Maybe you're in a sales job with a fear of rejection: there's a telephone in front of you, and you need to make calls . . . but the receiver starts to feel like it weighs 500 pounds, and you can't pick it up, no matter how hard you try. You're scared of the person on the other end saying no and rejecting you. Maybe you've forgotten that it's the *concept* you're selling that's being rejected rather than *you* as a person.

If you're in a sales position or something new that calls for you to make a phone call, or if you need to talk with somebody or make a presentation or anything of that kind, just remember that the people you're talking to don't have a script. Most of the time they don't know the things that you know, so your presentation material is probably brand new to them. *You* are the expert. The person on the other end of the phone doesn't already understand what you're going to say, and to be truthful, it's not that important. Besides, you need to practice on some people anyway. Don't think about the fear you have of making a fool of yourself. Just understand that some people are going to say no, and just think of them as "people you're practicing on."

I understand that the fear of rejection can be overwhelmingly powerful and real to you; I've been there myself, having spent most of my life in sales and business. I understand what rejection is. For me, rejection started much further back, much earlier in my life before I started working, and I understand that it probably did for a lot of other people too. In a sales capacity, rejection started when I sold plant seeds and greeting cards door-to-door when I was nine or ten years old. I had purchased these items myself, and the only way I would get my money back was if I sold them to people I didn't know. I had no intention of losing money; I couldn't afford it.

Also, I remember later going door to door when selling real estate asking people if they were interested in selling their home. That was tough at first but really what was the worst that could happen? Someone could shut the door in my face and I have to say, that didn't happen often. And some people loved to talk about real estate and as I got to know people more, because I would call on the same houses a couple of times a year or more and they would receive my newsletters, they actually became friendly. So that initial fear was really unfounded, but I will tell you that most realtors didn't go door to door, some did, but not many so my competition was very limited.

It's important that we rid ourselves of the shackles of fear and rejection because, really, with rejection comes strength. As long as you resolve that there is nothing to fear, it will only serve to make you a much stronger person. If you really stick with whatever you desire, your burning passion, then rejection is best used as fuel for your success.

In business, you can quantify rejection. When I was in real estate I learned to do this. I started with the average commission amount I would earn on each sale of a property, and I knew how many people I would need to talk with in order to get a presentation. I also knew how many presentations it would take for me to obtain a client that would result in a commission. So I would divide the number of contacts I made into the average commission I would make, and this allowed me to give each "no" a dollar value. This allowed me to turn rejection into a positive scenario because I knew the value of a no, and I knew that every no brought me closer to that payday: "yes."

If you're in sales, I challenge you to quantify a similar type of dollar amount for your personal situation. In advertising, they quantify the amount of money spent with the number of customers the campaign generates. This tells them the "cost of acquisition" of a new customer, and from there they can quantify the length of time a customer will remain with them, and how much that customer is likely to buy from them. That way they can quantify the cost accordingly, for example, if they spend $100 to get a customer and they sell $300 worth of product to them over a period of time, then they know they have a three to one return on their investment. Depending on their profit margins, this may or may not be a good return, but it allows them to put a value on acquisition.

You can do the same in sales or in any kind of business. Quantify what each "no" means to you, and then turn it around so that it becomes a positive. Honestly, what's the worst thing that could happen? If you think about it from this perspective, you will find that your fears are unfounded. It is better to have tried and failed than to never have tried at all. With each trial comes growth and learning. If you are to get ahead, it's critical that you step outside of your comfort zone. Let's face it, you've been too comfortable where you are for too long, and that's why you are now about halfway through this book . . . you want things to change, and you want to step away from the familiar place you're currently in.

At some point you will have to step outside your comfort zone. This will be part of your growth and part of your challenge. The thought of this may suddenly evoke all sorts of new fears within you, but don't panic. When I encourage you to step outside your comfort zone, I'm not asking you to leap outside of it immediately. You don't need to take big steps right away if you are not ready.

It's OK to take little steps to begin with, if that's all you can do right now. Like the old saying, "a dripping faucet still fills a bathtub," little steps to begin with are still steps that will take you away from your former existence and into a brighter and better future. For example, if you want to become a person who can speak confidently in front of a room of 200 people, you can start small by giving a presentation one-on-one to a friend, spouse, partner, or someone you know well, who will only give you positive feedback.

That can be step one, if you have this fear. Step two may be doing a presentation to three or four people and then in front of a small room of close friends and associates. That room size can grow and grow until you reach your goal of two hundred people. Just don't panic when you're asked to do something new; every journey begins with one first step.

Making a confident presentation comes with knowing your material inside out, from having practiced, and from taking action on visualizing yourself in front of that room of people. Another way to move yourself forward in the area of development is to pay less attention to yourself and more attention to your excellent message. Think about the message you're about to deliver to those people. You've put it down, and you know what you want to say. You've practiced it, and now it's just a matter of paying attention to the message you're providing, and making sure you provide value to your audience. Value does not have to be in monetary terms; it can be of value to people to receive information or knowledge that they didn't have before.

Another way to alleviate fear is to focus on the opportunities that come from each challenge. Within every challenge, there is an opportunity as long as you train yourself to look for it. Think about it: if you're faced with a challenge or an obstacle and you tell yourself "it's no good, I'm never going to be able to do this," then you are already on the wrong track. Whereas if you head off with the thought that you are going to give everything that comes your way your best possible effort, then you are automatically setting off a different set of responses in your brain. You are setting off positive neural pathways that tell you that you *can* achieve things.[9]

If you constantly focus on the negative things that have happened, then your brain will recall those first. Training and developing new neural pathways in your brain now will only set you up positively for the future. As we age, we must keep our brains active. People who do word puzzles or keep reading new things are training their brains to keep working long into old age. This can help to stave off the onset of certain kinds of dementia. Even something as simple as putting your left shoe on first instead of your right, or vice versa, opens up new pathways in the brain. If you tell your brain often enough that "you can and you will," it will remain a well-oiled and functioning machine. Your PPM will do the same thing, opening new pathways and helping to keep your brain fit and in good working order.

Many people face challenges on a daily basis and manage to turn them into opportunities, and we can all learn from that kind of grit and determination. Imagine being dyslexic and struggling just to make sense of what I'm saying to you. How on earth would you manage to get ahead in business if you couldn't understand written facts and figures? And yet, you may not even realize, there are many well-known people who were dyslexic, such as Ann Bancroft, Alexander Graham Bell, Loretta Young, George Washington, and Richard Branson to name but a few.

None of these people ever viewed life as being anything but a set of opportunities ready to be grabbed with both hands. Yes, they faced challenges along the way, but they managed to turn them into some of the greatest opportunities ever. That's something you will develop the power to do ... seize every opportunity that comes your way. Don't *not* do something because you're scared of the consequences. Always ask the crucial question: what's the worst that can happen?

When I was at a point in my life when I had no income or money, and really no place to turn to within the real estate market, given that sales had all but dried up and I had been shaken to the core by my bankruptcy, I needed to make a decision about what it was I was going to do with my life. I definitely felt a great deal of fear that I may not accomplish what I was setting out to do. But something changed within me when I started to employ the techniques I'm sharing with you: I became less fearful about my future and *more exhilarated* about where I was going. I had arrived at the stage where I could see it, I could feel it, and I knew it was a part of me. I knew it was going to happen.

To help eliminate fear and in order to succeed, in a sales situation or relationships, focus on the other person and providing benefit to them and being present to them in that moment. When you focus on them, you are not thinking about yourself and most fear is eliminated. Remember that most people are tuned into the radio station WIIFM: "What's In It For Me?" When you start to think from the prospective the other person's point of view; from *their* viewpoint about the presentation or impression you are making and service you're providing to them, you'll see a huge shift in their response. The same can be said about your job and providing your company or boss with your best possible service. They will usually take notice.

This is what happens when you try to tune in to their radio station and answer their question for them, "What's in it for me?" Once you can answer that question, you start to think on their level and give them what they want. And I consider this to be the whole point of being in business: giving the other person something they want, at a price which they feel is favorable to them but is also lucrative for you. That's when it becomes a win-win situation.

If you feel nervous about giving a presentation or if you get stuck when building a presentation, then get up from your desk and take a walk around the block. Simply get some fresh air and shift your thoughts to something you enjoy. Maybe you can imagine lying on a beach, or playing with your dog, or having a nice bottle of wine with your partner or friends. Think about something positive as you're taking your walk, and you will find that it re-energizes your thoughts and helps you to concentrate. Also, think about what the other person wants to hear from you in the presentation. An alternative for some people is doing push-ups or sit-ups instead of walking, which is fine also.

If you're feeling extra tired, don't be afraid to take a ten or fifteen minute nap on your break or in your chair, or just take a quick lie-down (if this is permitted in your office). You'll be surprised how much of a difference a short power nap can make to the rest of your day's production.

If you find yourself in a bit of a funk or a bad mood, then do something positive to get out of that state rather than brooding on it. Your visualization technique will be powerful in this case as well. And again, by taking breaks from tedious tasks, you can help to break that mood.

Different people will react in different ways to different things in order to change their moods from negative to positive. Personally, I love very upbeat music – something energetic, probably a little bit pop and a lot of fun. It really gets the blood pumping for me. When I do my exercises, this is the type of music I like listening to because it stimulates my mind in a powerful and positive way, and that in turn motivates me to work harder. So if I ever find myself in a bit of a funk, I turn on a playlist that I know gets me going. Just remember that positive thinking is an important aspect of your success plan, but without action, positive thinking is nothing. And without visualization, positive thinking is nothing.

If you were able to visualize that tomato, then you also have the ability to visualize your life. Remember, there's nothing to fear but fear itself, and remember our key question: "What's the worst thing that could happen?" Usually very little. Persistence will overcome in most cases. Give every roadblock you encounter one more try every time, as many times as necessary, with enthusiasm and conviction.

Your efforts will become *amazing* accomplishments when you do this. As we talk more about visualizing your future and creating it in your mind, understand that we're not talking about *living* in the future, in and of itself. We're talking about *creating* your future.

We can live and act today in order to create our desired results in the future. Successful people understand that roadblocks exist; however, they don't allow themselves to dwell on them. They focus on the future and the positive results they want to achieve. Each deliberate positive action taken on a daily basis leads to the results they envision.

In the next chapter, I will show you how to positively visualize the creation of your future, and as we talk about it, you will see your future begin to manifest itself and learn why it will automatically be drawn to you.

Stay committed to your decisions,

but stay flexible in your approach.

Tony Robbins

SIX

IT'S YOUR UNIVERSE – MAKE IT!

In the last chapter, we talked about how positive thinking alone is *not* the key to success in and of itself. Of course, positive thinking is helpful and powerful; however, success takes more than just positive thinking. We also did our first visualization exercise, about "seeing" a simple tomato being sliced. This kind of visualization will become the basis and foundation for creating *everything* that you want to achieve. As you begin to achieve your goals and objectives, those things you truly desired, expected, and envisioned will actually manifest themselves in your life. You will find you will not only *achieve* your goals, but you will achieve them easily and simply because as you visualize and expect these goals to manifest in your life, they will actually start to occur.

Of course, we accept that our world is governed by the laws of the universe and physics. For example, the Law of the Conservation states that energy cannot be created or destroyed, only transformed. And we know that everything is made of vibrating electrons and neutrons. Even things which appear solid are, in fact, constantly moving. This is the (soft) Law of Vibration. Why is this important? Well, in the context of this book, we will adapt the use and consequences of these laws to engage with the significant powers of the Laws of Attraction, Relativity and Abundance, to state just a couple of them. Although not exactly provable in the scientific world, I have seen them take effect time and time again. I have faith that they not only exist but that they are around us always. And here we choose to utilize them for our benefit.

When you put these concepts together, you realize that the universe has everything there, just waiting for you to find a way to plug into it, to find a way to attract these goals into your life. Utilizing the techniques in this book, and your PPM, plugs you into that power so you become a magnet, attracting everything you desire. Once you get "plugged in" to that universal energy, that power, those vibrations, you will be in tune with the elements of the universe, which will allow you to create anything that you truly desire. If this is the first time you're hearing or learning this, you may think I am talking crazy. You might think, "This guy is off his rocker." But I assure you, these techniques work. I have seen it in my own life and the lives of many people.

Many people have believed in these "soft" laws of the universe for a long, long time. Ralph Waldo Emerson referred to it as the "Law of Compensation." If you want to make something good happen in your life, then you need to figure out what action will cause it to happen, and then take that action. Conversely, if there is something bad happening that you want to prevent, then you need to figure out what action is causing it to happen and take steps to stop that action. The correct application of some of these laws can change your life forever.

Believe it or not, some of these soft laws go back as far as 2000 BC, when they were written by the ancient Egyptians.[10] They've also been the subject of many thousands of books throughout the centuries. If you're absolutely determined to achieve everything on your list and to be the best you can be, then you're already halfway there by reading this book. These laws – such as gravity – *are in motion*, regardless of whether you have knowledge of or belief in them or utilize them to your benefit. These laws almost always govern the way your life will evolve, and you can be certain that these universal soft laws are always there, always in operation. They're not going to turn on and off at your will. For example, the law of gravity will continue to work even if you fall down a cliff; wishing against gravity is not going to stop it from being there!

Understanding these laws and their power will enable you to make better choices. And in making better choices, you will be driving your life to its fullest capabilities. The Law of Abundance is an interesting one. In *Little Money Bible: the Ten Laws of Abundance*, Stuart Wilde states that it is our "birth right" to be wealthy and explains ten laws to make his case.[11] I explain this law in this way, no matter which way you look, abundance is the norm everywhere in nature; abundance is the *rule*. Plants and animals are prolific in nature and at the same time there are ebbs and flows due to other natural occurrences like fires and floods. Nature is usually in balance when not interfered with by humans. Our job is to allow that abundance to come to us and to embrace it, to expect it and to just be OK with it.

Think about everything around you: there are trillions of cells making up your body, trillions of seeds present in a forest, and an unimaginable number of hydrogen molecules making up the sun. The creation of what we manifest in life begins with thoughts, and therefore anything is made possible by cultivating the right thoughts. I have seen that the universe doesn't differentiate between your thoughts on your behalf. If you focus on what is lacking in your life and get caught up in negativity, then expect to attract that right back at you, and in abundance. However, if you focus on gaining the success you are after, and having good things in your life, then those are the very things you'll attract, also in abundance. It's therefore a must to get yourself in harmony with all that's possible in the universe. We do this by focusing on what we want in our lives. Your PPM does exactly that.

The Law of Cause and Effect states that everything in this world happens for a reason and that for every cause there is an effect and for every effect there is a cause.[12] Everything that has occurred thus far in your life (the effects) has happened because of something you did or didn't do (the causes). Understand that your mind is the strongest and most powerful "cause" that exists in this world. If you remember, I began this book by pointing out that we are where we are as a result of all of the past decisions we have made. Your inner thoughts and your world within yourself are what will bring about change in your external circumstances. You will use the Law of Cause and Effect to create change within yourself. Change means moving from being a *victim* of circumstance to being a *creator* of circumstance; there's a huge difference in a single word, from "victim" to "creator." You can use this law to its best effect by being selective and careful when you choose your thoughts and the visions you will use to program your subconscious mind.

When you think carefully about the things you want and attach emotion to them, they begin to manifest in your life. Inexorably and almost inevitably, the world outside you will reward you with the gifts you've already focused on in your thoughts.

Another law to consider here is the Law of Growth. The Big Bang took place some 13.8 billion years ago, and it is generally accepted that since that momentous occasion, the universe has continued to grow. In fact, it was recently proven that the growth rate of the universe is actually accelerating, where as several years back it was thought, but not proven, that the universe was shrinking.[13] In essence, you are like the universe and will continue to grow throughout your life, but it's *how* you grow that's important, and not just in a physiological way. You're probably aware that cells in the body grow and die every day of your life. In fact, within any seven-year period, there will not be a single cell in your body that has not been renewed since the start of that time-span.

Learn to recognize that events that have happened in your life have happened for a reason. That reason is growth, knowingly or unknowingly. Some of us choose to learn from things that have happened, and some choose to dismiss the lesson; the choice is yours. You may have already noticed that certain circumstances keep repeating in your life. You may have had similar break-ups in relationships or always felt that you never have enough money. If this sounds familiar, you may want to take note of the lesson the universe is trying to give you. Ask yourself, "What do I need to learn, both for my spiritual and physical well-being?" By doing this, you will open yourself up to transcending the shackles that hold you back in your current way of thinking.

In the Law of Relativity, we perceive things as being good or bad, relative to something else; we need to use a "yardstick" for comparison. It's your thinking, however, that makes a situation seem good or bad. Shifting your viewpoint can make a situation appear very different. Perceptions of a situation can also vary if you think about it: two minutes can seem interminable if you're waiting for the bathroom to become free. Conversely, those same two minutes can disappear in a flash when you're doing something you enjoy, such as walking along a sandy beach with loved ones. The Law of Relativity, also means we will be in circumstances that are beyond our control, even though the decisions we made got us to that place or point. At that juncture we must let go of what might have just happened, the event or whatever it was and get back to using our PPM to move toward our objectives. Some say "everything happens for a reason" and this is what they are talking about. Be "OK" with it and if you figure out the reason, great. If not, don't dwell and move on, things become clear with time.

We all find ourselves in challenging circumstances now and again, but you can utilize the Law of Relativity to assist you in feeling and perceiving things in a different way. A lot of people think about how much worse things could be, but switch that around and think about how you would prefer life to be. Remember the Law of Attraction; you don't want to focus on the bad stuff!

Several people may be in very similar situations, but they may emerge from them having had completely different experiences, just because their focuses differed and they kept focused on their objectives. You need to take charge of how you perceive your circumstances. If you find that your feelings don't empower you, then they aren't supporting you, and you need to change them.

The Law of Polarity helps us understand that for every action there is a reaction; in other words, there is an opposite of everything.

Take comfort in the fact that if something bad happens to you, you can rest assured that, according to the Law of Polarity, which states that everything has an opposite, something good also exists in these circumstances.[14] However, it might be up to you to find the good. Don't feel hindered or trapped by thinking things are only black or white; never forget that there are many different shades of gray along the spectrum. Rarely is something an either/or choice. Learn to explore the many different potential outcomes that can, and do, exist between two different choices.

The Law of Manifestation states that just as time takes its course when a seed incubates, sprouts, and grows, the same is true of your thoughts. Maybe you're already using the above laws and are now getting frustrated with the speed at which things are changing. Accept that you are in the "pregnancy" stage. Have patience while you continue to work toward your goals, and eventually you'll give "birth" to that which you're focused on. Have faith in the Law of Manifestation.

Although your current reality may be an empty bank account, low self-esteem, or lack of sales in your chosen profession, you don't want to let that get in the way of your future success; you cannot allow that to happen. Your PPM moves you through the position you're currently in and helps you create a new belief system for yourself; in fact, your PPM helps you create a complete new reality for yourself. In order to create the reality, however, we must first create the *thought*, create the *plan*, and then start moving in the direction of your new reality.

We've already created the first aspects of your strong foundation with the exercises you have done to this point. From here we are going to build upon everything you've done up to this point. You're *not* going to let past results dictate what your future results will be, because they just don't matter. What's done is done.

Remember, you are now looking forward and not back. When you put in practice the methodology, you'll find that things that happened in the past just don't matter. Even the failures from which you learned a lesson don't matter. Accept that you have had learning experiences, but from now on, you're going to create positive movement toward all the objectives you set for yourself. You will see that training your conscious and subconscious mind to move you toward your goals and objectives is really quite simple, but it may not always be easy: a commitment is required. But anything worth doing requires a commitment.

You won't be forcing your way toward these things, but merely moving yourself in a positive direction. This movement will become easier and easier as you become more proficient at employing the techniques.

Some people often have a tendency to allow their thought patterns to be negative ones, but the interesting thing about the subconscious mind is that it can be trained both negatively and positively. It has the ability to bring to life whatever your dominant thoughts are, what you picture *most often* in your conscious mind. With your PPM, we will be reprogramming your subconscious so that you're moving forward and taking appropriate and positive action to get you where you want to go.

When you see the results and develop a certainty that you can program your subconscious mind, you become unbeatable and unstoppable. You'll find that you have no limitations. You'll be able to do things and accomplish things that, in the past, you would never have been able to imagine achieving.

Some of the negative thoughts that may still persist in your mind might stem from things that you don't like doing, things you really feel that you would rather not do. They could be mundane chores such as painting a fence, cleaning the bathroom, or any other household chore. Maybe you don't enjoy washing your car or being the magic laundry fairy who cleans, dries, irons and carefully makes it all appear back in its proper place! Believe me, we are all alike when it comes to such chores. Most of us don't actually want to be doing them, but we understand that they must be done. There may be things in your life that you don't particularly like doing, but when you think logically, you know they have to be accomplished. Perhaps one of the reasons you have been scared of moving forward is that you fear hurting someone, or doing something else that you don't like the idea of.

Certain things in life must be done, whether we like it or not. If this means disassociating yourself from someone who is holding you back, well, so be it. This doesn't mean that you are a bad or cruel person; it just means that you are taking the necessary steps to a better life for yourself and your family. Just remember, no one else will look after your interests in the same way you can and should. If they had the courage and foresight to know what their futures could hold, many people would do what you are about to do, rather than remaining in the ruts they are currently in.

I recommend for the chores and other activities you really don't like to do, make it one of your goals to pay others to do them for you, freeing our mind and my time for things that are important to you. This, in turn, helps you move toward the things that you really enjoy doing. Of course, money is necessary, but as you start to achieve more success, you'll also be able to pay someone else to do the tasks you choose not to do.

You will discover that your time has become much more valuable than the few dollars you would spend to have your house cleaned, your car cleaned, or your fence painted. As your income and your hourly value begin to increase, you'll find that it actually becomes less productive for you to do these routine activities.

Our brains are bombarded every day with messages, both positive *and* negative, from lots of different sources. Whether you're at work with colleagues, or even watching or listening to advertising on the radio and television, we're all constantly being bombarded with unnecessary and unproductive messages. So it's important that we train our subconscious to rid itself of those messages and that we fill our minds with the kind of messages we want to be acting on.

Instead of letting those random messages enter your brain and dictate your direction in life, from now on, *you* are going to be responsible for dictating the messages that go into your brain. You can create your future, and in turn, create your success.

Your PPM is key to helping you create the behaviors you want to employ in your life. These behaviors are the action steps you will use to create your success. Forming clear pictures in your mind will be the most effective way to advance yourself quickly toward your goals, because you'll be able to work more effectively and intelligently than your supposed competitors do.

Once you understand that, there's very little competition in this world. Many people don't work very hard at their jobs. It's relatively easy to stand out and look much better than someone else who works *just* hard enough that the company won't fire them. In return, the company pays them *just* enough so that they won't leave. After all, hiring someone else would be an additional cost to the company; training someone else can be very expensive. Hence, you don't have to work that much harder or even be that much smarter than your colleagues, to get ahead. It's going to come down to your desires, your expectations, and how clearly you create the vision of what you want to accomplish in your life. Desire without expectation or action is nothing more than wishful thinking.

Part of becoming successful is learning how to manage time, as time is one of the finite things we need to work with. Just as we all live by the same universal laws, so too do we all have the same number of minutes and hours in a day. How effectively do you use that time?

At the moment, you may feel as if you don't have enough hours in the day and that you are constantly on the go, but is it possible that some of your time could be better spent on other pursuits? How do you quantify that? How can you tell if you are spending unnecessary time on unnecessary tasks?

As your income improves, you will be able to employ others to do things you don't enjoy doing, but until that time comes, you need to identify how you spend your time so that you can see how best to make changes. It becomes critical to identify your priorities and the time wasters so you can make good use of your available time.

In chapter four, when you wrote down everything you did in five minute segments, did you realize how you were really spending your time? How much time was being wasted or was unproductive? If you haven't analyzed that data yet, now is the moment to do so. Look at the records of that week and be honest with yourself. In that week, how much time were you actually doing unproductive things? Were those large segments, or was your unproductive time just a few minutes here and there? Can you see where you can find more time for something productive that moves you toward your goals? I generally find that when people do this exercise, they find a minimum of thirty minutes a day that they can use more effectively to move toward their objectives. Often, if you are totally honest with yourself, you have far more than thirty minutes you could be using better.

Of course, it's important that you also factor in time for yourself, a time where it is OK to do absolutely nothing and relax. We all need to recharge the batteries, but try to make sure that all essential tasks are completed before you think about having your downtime.

Take note of how much time you waste at work. Maybe you spend five spare minutes here and there surfing the internet, answering personal emails, and other things like that. These are all important time-wasters to identify. A lot of people are genuinely shocked at how much time is wasted rather than used productively. Use each and every moment with purpose, even if that purpose is to chill out.

It's when we spend time thoughtlessly that we stagnate and move backwards. If you have a spare fifteen minutes and want to spend that time relaxing, great! You've identified that you need a break, so you are using your time wisely. Do you see the difference now?

If you can't be honest with yourself about what you're doing today, then how will you go about making the changes that will get you where you want to go? For example, when managing your time, be precise in your scheduling: if you have an appointment at 1:00 p.m. and it takes you twenty minutes to get there, don't schedule it in your calendar at 1:00 p.m. Put it in your diary at 12:40 because you know you must be in your car driving by that time. Maybe there's another twenty or thirty minutes of preparation involved in making this appointment a fruitful one, so you should also schedule the time required to allow for your preparation.

This is how effective time management can make a huge difference in your life if you want to start to create something over and above what you're currently doing. Maybe you think you haven't got time to start your own business or do something else on the side that will create additional wealth in your life. You need to find some additional time, and by using the information you gained when you logged your week, you will probably be able to see how and where you can do that.

Like attracts like, as we have talked about, so you'll want to be hanging out with like-minded people who are of good intention and good integrity. Figure out ways you can help others to help you achieve your dreams. Bring something extra into your life by reading quality books and watching quality television and movies; take a break from reading trashy novels or watching trashy television.

No one is saying that you can't have downtime, but put that time to good use by learning something that's going to move you toward your goals. Become a good listener. Listening is an amazing attribute; as you listen, ideas start to formulate in your mind and sometimes it's good to be silent. Don't feel you have to fill the silences; use that time to be thoughtful and soak up what another person has been saying.

When you're around new situations, it's great to be involved in the conversation, but make sure not to dominate the chatter, just participate. In sales situations, it is always better to be asking questions of your prospect so you can learn what they are after and fill that need for them with your product or opportunity. And whomever is asking the questions is in control of the conversation.

Listening is, unfortunately, often undervalued as a skill. The ability to listen accurately means that you not only receive messages properly, but you have a better chance of interpreting them correctly. This only serves to enhance the whole process of communication. Listening is the key to enjoying effective communication. If you don't practice your ability to listen effectively, then the messages you do receive could easily be misunderstood. That's when communication breaks down, and the person talking might become irritated or frustrated.

We were given two ears

and one mouth for a reason.

Anonymous

In fact, learning how to listen is so important that many top employers actually provide training in the art of listening. It's really not that surprising when you acknowledge that good listening skills can improve customer satisfaction, generate greater productivity with fewer mistakes being made, and increase the sharing of information, which in turn leads to more innovative ideas and fresh work being produced.

Many successful business entrepreneurs will tell you that their success can be credited, in part, to having effective listening skills. Richard Branson is often quoted as saying that "Listening is one of the main factors behind the success of Virgin." Productive listening is a necessary skill that can underpin all kinds of positive human relationships. Spend some time thinking about your listening skills; consider the idea that listening carefully to what is *not* being said can be just as important as hearing what is said. Learning to recognize body language can be a great tool in the psychology of selling and in business. Spend time developing your listening skills; they are the building blocks of continued success.

As you improve your listening skills and your conscious visualization skills, you'll find that things are beginning to come your way. The universe will be opening up and creating opportunities for you because there's nothing in this world that stands still. Remember: if you're not moving forward, you're moving backward.

As your subconscious mind begins to work on moving you toward your objectives, everything will start to fall into place one way or another. Of course, you need to be taking action, and action requires decision. Indecision creates confusion in the brain, and you won't know which direction to move in. Therefore, you must make decisions and act upon them in order to move yourself forward. And do so without fear.

Fear stifles our thinking and actions.

It creates indecisiveness that results in stagnation.

I have known talented people who procrastinate

indefinitely rather than risk failure.

Lost opportunities cause erosion of confidence,

and the downward spiral begins.

Charles F. Stanley

We are now moving on to the most exciting part of the book, one I know you are going to be eager to get into. In the next chapter we're going to further explore how to attract various facets of your life wishes and goals toward you and start to formalize exactly what it is that you're after. I can't wait to get started; can you?

Formal education will make you a living;

self-education will make you a fortune.

Jim Rohn

SEVEN

BE A GOAL MAGNET

In chapter six we talked about how everything you need to achieve success already exists in the universe. In this chapter, we will further explore the laws we live by. Why am I spending so much time on these laws? Because we don't have a choice as to whether or not we live by them. They are one of the few things in life we can't choose. However, the good news is that we can use these laws, these forces, to our personal advantage. We just need to tap in to them, and that is exactly what your PPM will do for you.

We also talked about how harnessing the power of the universal laws enables us to utilize them to create the things we desire in our lives. We're going to take this a step further and talk about using those laws to become a "goal magnet." You will literally be able draw your goals toward you. You will write them down with a specific message to yourself in order to make them real and give yourself something tangible to focus on.

The Harvard Business School ran a study on the financial status of its students ten years after they had graduated. The results, as discussed in Michael Masterson's 2010 book *The Pledge*, may surprise you: 27 percent of the prestigious institution's former students needed financial assistance, 60 percent were living paycheck to paycheck, 10 percent were living comfortably, and only 3 percent were financially independent.[15] Furthermore, and here's where the findings get very interesting, they found the 27 percent who required financial assistance had no goal-setting process in their lives. The 60 percent who were living paycheck to paycheck only had basic survival goals like how to manage their bank accounts or paychecks. The 10 percent who were living comfortably knew where they were going, and they had plans or pictures of where they wanted to be five years from that time. Most striking, however, were the people who were financially independent: that 3 percent had written down goals and the steps required to reach them.

The results of that study show that in order to achieve your goals, it's not only necessary to have those goals set clearly in your mind, but also have in place the action steps that are needed to reach them. This confirms what we've discussed up to this point. Early on in my real estate days, I used a day planner as my time planner and found it to be very effective tool for me. You can find some very good insights on time management on the website daytimer.com.

This isn't just a book on goal setting. I am showing you exactly what I did to reach my own goals and how you can do exactly the same. Understand that when you're writing your goals out, the words you use are also highly relevant. You want to write in a specific way so that the ideas will transpose themselves from your conscious to your subconscious mind. That way your subconscious mind will immediately start to work on them, which in turn will help them to manifest in your life in ways you hadn't even considered. Most of the time people attract things into their life by accident rather than by choice. If we look at some of the definitions of the terms or ideas we're going to be using, you'll start to specifically develop what it is that you're going to achieve.

Let me illustrate what I mean by the word choice. In the examples below, I'm using just one of the dictionary definitions when there are maybe three or four, but that choice is purposeful.

You are either performing simple disciplines that are moving you closer to your preferred reality, or simple errors in judgment that are moving you away from your preferred reality.

Jim Rohn

Plan is "a specific project or definite purpose." What does that tell us? It reiterates that a plan is something *specific* and something *with purpose*. That's interesting when we put it in context alongside the other aspects of your future we're currently looking at.

Goal is "the result or achievement toward which effort is directed; aim or end." When you think about it, that is exactly what you're after, and soon we'll direct your efforts toward that goal. That definition is right in line with what we've been talking about already.

Daydream is "a vision voluntarily indulged in while awake." Of course, dreams also happen when we're asleep; that's when your subconscious mind is doing a great deal of work as you head towards your goals. However, note that the dictionary said, *while awake*. This means you can picture something at your will, while awake. You are manifesting this dream, this vision yourself, and by doing so you are training your subconscious to make it reality. To move you toward what you want to achieve, and to have what you want to achieve move toward you.

Task is "a definite piece of work expected of a person." These daily tasks are going to be ones that you set for yourself to accomplish. When we put it all together, we have a plan, we have a goal, we have a dream, and we have a task. Each day your tasks will be moving you incrementally toward your goals.

From my previous experience, I can tell you that everything will start with your waking dream or vision, your daydream. From that vision, you'll set your goal or goals, and then you'll set the plan, followed by the tasks required to fulfill that plan and attain your goal. These four elements meld together to create everything in your life that you are after today.

Before we move on to the next stage of your plan, it's crucial for you to decide specifically what is important to you. This is not the time to be vague or unsure. In chapter two I asked you to write out everything that you would like to accomplish or do in your life. Now I want you to be extremely specific. You can't just say, "I want a lot of money. I want ten million dollars." Acquiring wealth is a great goal, however, you need to think specifically about what that money is going to do for you. Look at the list you have created and start to choose which you want first and when. Be precise. You need to get very specific about the things you want to accomplish and when; pin it down.

It is essential that when you start to write out your goals and create your PPM that you phrase your ideas in positive statements that are active in nature. These statements will take you toward everything you want to attain. The exercise in this chapter is for you look at the list you have created and take from it everything you want to accomplish in the next two years – just the next twenty-four months.

CHAPTER SEVEN EXERCISE

What do you want to accomplish in the next two years? Consider the following categories and write the specifics: your health, your bank account, your money, your personal development, and your relationships.

If you are in sales, how many sales are you going to make in the coming year, and what income will they provide you? Are you going to start a new part-time business? Do you know what kind? If not, you decide on a process, and make it a goal to pick or find a business idea.

Think about these areas even more carefully: everything you are wanting during the next twenty-four months. Once you have made that list, write down two to three tasks per goal, it will take to achieve the goals you have set for yourself. Some goals may be more complex and require more than three tasks. This information will be the foundation of your PPM. Also make one-year, three-year, five-year, and seven-year goals. Personally, I like thee-year goals because the time frame is close enough that you really grasp it.

Next, determine the steps that will lead you to your two-year goal. Where will you be in one year to be on track for your two-year goal? What about in six months? This should include markers along the way and a list of the tasks you need to accomplish your objectives. Look at your goals and work backwards to determine the tasks that will be required to get there, and write those out as well. The tasks are of course very important. Determine these with as much detail as you can. We'll discuss this more when you are actually creating your PPM.

Starting from wherever you are, within seven years, you should be able to create whatever manner of lifestyle you would like for yourself, and it can even be done more quickly than that. I really want you to hear this message: you can achieve a massive change in your life within one year, and within five to seven years you can become completely financially free.

As you develop your plan and implement the tasks within it, your faith in your ability to accomplish all this will start to grow. As you program your subconscious, your ability to achieve greater accomplishments will increase. That's not to say that you won't have setbacks. You may encounter roadblocks that deter you or slightly alter your route. But that's OK; with persistence and your PPM you will, eventually, accomplish what you set out to do, and you can overcome whatever complications are placed in your path.

You'll start to attract everything you need in your life, and these things will come in ways that you never expected and may not recognize. They'll come from out of nowhere! Recently, I was talking to a friend with whom I had worked many years ago and with whom I hadn't spoken in a few years. He was attempting to get an anti-bullying program implemented in his local school system and ideally province-wide. He was in touch with a specific politician whom I happen to know personally, and my friend needed another voice to advocate for him.

After a short discussion, I understood his situation, and I sent an email to the politician. Within twenty-four hours, the politician and my friend had scheduled a meeting. Before we spoke, my friend didn't know how he was going to get a meeting with this particular person. He knew that he wanted a meeting and had established some initial contact, but had no idea if such a meeting would ever actually take place.

My friend personally understands and uses the techniques we're discussing here. He had put it out to the universe that he needed something to fall into place for him, and as it turned out, my random call helped him do just that. This is the Law of Attraction in a nutshell!

Additionally, my friend was selling a business that he'd had for several years, and he was looking for another business to start or get involved with. We're now working together again, on one of my businesses. This is very exciting as are these two significant pursuits in both our lives. All that from an out-of-the-blue phone call that the universe somehow knew should be made by me.

You'll recall that one of the most important aspects of the Law of

Attraction is the fact that you can attract both the positive and the negative. As the saying goes, "Be careful what you wish for, because you just might get it." Here are a few more points to consider about attracting positivity and negativity into your life. Be sure to read carefully; this could change your outlook and, ultimately, your life:

Attracting positively remarkable things into your life is a simple process, provided that you embark on it with thought and discernment. But you should also be aware that the Laws of Attraction can be perilous if you don't take care in your approach.

"Talk is cheap," and this is never truer than when you are in denial about whether the Law of Attraction is real. The real power of the Law of Attraction comes from a deeper place within your subconscious; you can meditate for weeks to no avail if you are not using the correct language for your programming. If you still don't have a strong belief in this Law, don't worry, as you use your PPM you will see it in action.

Even if, at this moment, you think this is all bunk, fine, but if you complete the process, you will experience the reality and the results. Make yourself a believer because it is truly worth it. Now the power of visualization really comes into play. Picturing yourself living the kind of life you wish for is the greatest way to start. Finding parking spots in a busy mall as I mentioned in chapter three is another small example of expectation and the Law of Attraction.

To take this one step further, make a "vision board" or some tangible collage of what you most desire in life. Take photos of the car you dream of owning. Go to the dealership, sit in it, and have your photo taken. Collect pictures of the style of property you dream about, and create a "perfect life" collage for yourself. Cut out words and phrases you've seen in magazines and newspapers that inspire you. Look at your collage or board every chance you get. Hang it somewhere prominent where your eyes can constantly be on it. Picture yourself sitting in the driver's seat, cooking in the sumptuous kitchen, or lying on the beach you want to experience. Make it a screen saver for your computer.

Be wary of developing negative obsessions. Sure, the universe is powerful and accommodating and wants you to be happy, but if you're obsessing about something, it is difficult for your subconscious to discern between the things you really want and those you don't. If you are stuck thinking that your life is awful or being afraid of losing your home or your partner, do you realize what could happen? The Law of Attraction can cause the very thing you don't want to actually happen.

Trust in the Law of Attraction working in the way it is meant to. It goes far deeper than your desire for more wealth, a new car, or a vacation. It will fuel you with what you need most in order to live the life you're meant to be living.

This brings us back to focusing on and developing your subconscious so that it takes you toward the things you want to accomplish in your life. As I said, the laws of physics are absolute and, as such, unchangeable and the soft laws we have been talking about are just as powerful. As you train your subconscious brain and start to put your message out into the universe, you will be amazed by what starts to happen in your life.

My earlier examples of finding parking spots and that fortuitous phone call to my friend are just the beginning. I was creating a marketing program recently, and one of the people who worked for me moved on to another project. Initially, I was concerned because he had been integral in the process. But within two days, I found someone even more qualified in the area of expertise I needed, and he actually found a number of flaws in the program we had created. This happened because I was focused on finding the right person for what I needed, and I quickly let go of the fact that I had been left unexpectedly short-handed. And even though my initial employee choice was wrong, it all worked out better than I expected. I was plugged into the universe, and I allowed it to bring me exactly who I needed most at that moment.

Spiritual people often talk about being "in synch" with the universe. Some people also feel that being in synch with the universe means being "in synch" with a god of a particular religion, and that's fine too. Although this feeling of being in synch can relate to spirituality, when it comes to creating success or wealth, using the universal Laws of Attraction just makes your job of acquiring what you're after that much easier. You most definitely have the ability to attract into your life whatever it is you want. You achieve this with positive expectations, positive actions, and positive visualizations.

Unlike sharpening one edge of a sword, this is much more a multifaceted diamond or object that you must learn to work with. Only then can you create and manifest what you want in your life. During your visualization, brainwaves are produced according to the positive or negative thoughts and pictures in our mind.[16] These brainwaves, or brain vibrations, take place constantly whether you are consciously thinking about something or not. In fact, everything is in a constant state of vibration. Everything is constantly moving because the molecules and atoms within it are constantly vibrating. Nothing, even if it appears solid, is actually solid. This brings us to another law, the Law of Vibration. We're not going to get into that, but I would like you to understand that it's all part of being in tune and plugging in to the universal power energy that's waiting there for you.

Have you ever noticed when certain people walk into a room and the room just seems to light up? Suddenly a new and unique energy is apparent in the room. People might say, "That person has a magnetic personality." That's the effect of the Laws of Vibration and Attraction. That person who lights up the room is putting out positive energy because they've manifested positive energy from within and from the universal energy around us all. They really do have a magnetic personality!

The process you are going to use and are using will enable you to become a goal magnet by placing your dreams, wishes, aspirations, and goals into your subconscious mind. This will allow your mind, through your actions, to work toward and manifest these things in ways you would never have thought were possible. While the results may seem coincidental at first, you will quickly come to know, deep within yourself, that this is not coincidence. It's the result of what you're putting out and what you are programming. I've seen it happen, and I know it works. It's happened for me time and time again, and these powers and laws have helped me create a multi-million-dollar business. You can do it too!

You can become that person who lights up the room when you walk into it, the person who attracts positive people and positive circumstances toward themselves. You'll develop a sense of self-assurance and confidence like never before which will take you to new heights you didn't think possible before now. This isn't arrogance. It's not self-serving or egotistical. You will start to have self-confidence that is well founded because you will have a healthy, positive picture of yourself.

Don't forget you can also create the negative. We see this all the time. You might have already noticed it in celebrities sometimes. Their need to be wanted and liked is so important to them that they act out, do drugs, or do other stupid things. Yes, they create attention for themselves, but that attention is negative. It's not my intention to pick on celebrities, but these unfortunate circumstances exemplify the negative possibilities for the Law of Attraction.

Young children do the same thing when they want attention. They don't necessarily care if it's negative or positive. If children are not getting the positive attention they would like, they'll often do something just to get any type of attention, and often that attention is negative. To them, attention is attention. But if young children learn they can get attention through bad behavior, they will continue to do the same thing over and over. Obviously, this is not a healthy way to get attention.

When you're setting your goals, remember to include your fitness goals. Make time in your schedule for working out, either going to the gym or exercising at home. I know I've talked about this already, but being healthy is very, very important. Did you know that flossing your teeth can protect you against heart disease, diabetes, and other health issues?[17] Something as simple as having good gums actually makes you healthier. It's a small and simple thing, but all too often, people simply don't take it seriously. They don't believe that something as simple as your gums can have such a huge impact on heart health. Though it may seem irrelevant, I suggest including a few minutes in your daily schedule to floss your teeth. It's tiny, yes, but hugely significant. Why would you not make an extra three minutes in your day for that?

POSITIVE PEOPLE SITUATIONS

I would like you to think about how you feel when you go to a retail store or supermarket and the cashier or salesperson is genuinely friendly. They're doing it because that's who they are. How do you feel when you have an encounter like that with a salesperson? Does it make you want to go back and do business with them again? It sure does for me, and I would be far more likely to recommend that store to my friends and family.

What are those salespeople doing? What are they actually doing at that moment? Are they attracting positive or negative feelings towards themselves? Of course they're attracting positive feelings towards themselves, so the likelihood of something positive coming from their actions is very strong. In fact, who knows, they may serve somebody one day who likes their attitude so much, that they get offered a job somewhere else at a higher pay or a better position. Great opportunities will start to come their way.

It's amazing what can happen: something as simple as being kind and friendly to another person can lead to great changes in your life. To take it a step further: if you find someone in your life who is bothersome, make a point of not spending time with that person. By doing this, you allow your subconscious to focus on creating what you want in your life rather than having to fend off negativity and bad behavior from other people. It comes down to being harmonious in everything that you do and once again getting in tune with the universe you want to create for yourself. This harmony also means getting in synch (when we are considering vibration) with what is going on around your life.

In addition to moving aside people who may be dragging you down, you might want to consider getting rid of things that you don't need any more – unnecessary things that are dragging you down, filling your closet, or just taking up space.

Think of your mind as being your mental closet. At least once a year, I go through my closet and get rid of clothing that I no longer wear by giving it to people in need. This clearing out not only creates much more space in my closet, but also my subconscious starts to recognize that, "I need some new clothes. I need a new shirt. I need a new pair of pants." I can fill the space I've created by finding a great shirt or a great outfit I wasn't even aware I wanted. I strongly recommend getting rid of items and accessories that clutter your life. Make room for the good; make room for the new.

By creating that vacuum, you make space for your subconscious to go to work for you. It's amazing how your brain will go about filling the spaces you have in your life. Of course, clothing is just an example. Conscious cleansing can be about any aspect of your life because that's the power of the subconscious. Wait and see what it will do for you and with you.

Your subconscious will start to create the reality that you are already envisioning, and as you become the person you want to be and start doing things without expecting anything in return, you'll be amazed at what will come back to you. Rewards will come your way through avenues that you'd never previously thought possible. And even though you can't change the universal laws, you *can* use them and empower them to create and manifest the things that you are seeking in your life.

In the next chapter, we're going to talk about being a little bit better, and how being a little better can create amazing amounts of additional wealth and prosperity in your life. Don't forget to do the chapter seven exercise in detail before moving on to chapter eight. Be specific and remember that the universe wants to give you what is best for you.

To dream by night is to escape your life. To dream by day is to make it happen.

Stephen Richards

EIGHT

THE RAZOR'S EDGE ~~THEORY~~ REALITY

In the last chapter, we talked about attracting the things you want to your life. We also looked at how, by plugging into the power of the universe and taking advantage of universal laws of energy, you can begin to have things manifest in your life, often in unexpected ways. We've also talked about the importance of keeping a daily journal which I will get to in a couple of paragraphs. First I want to talk about the title I've chosen for this chapter

I first heard about the Razor's Edge Theory when I read the book *You Are Born Rich*, by Bob Proctor. I found it extremely interesting and started to change a few things I did in my life. One simple Razor's Edge technique can literally put millions of dollars in your pocket. By starting your day a little earlier – possibly before other people around you – you can spend a productive hour or two without any interference, and without having anyone else in your space. You can do far more when it's early, and it's peaceful, and you can concentrate. Particularly if you have children.

But, I use "Reality" instead of "Theory" because I have proven to myself that it is far more than a theory. When you employ this reality, you will be head and shoulders ahead of your supposed competition.

The Razor's Edge Reality means that the people who are paid significantly larger amounts of money than you are not necessarily better than you. Think of baseball: a superstar batting average in baseball is about .300, or a little more. If you can hit consistently at .300, you're going to do extremely well. You're going to be paid huge sums of money for hitting the ball and getting on base safely only three out of every ten times at bat. Those who hit the ball safely two and a half times out of every ten – a batting average of .250 – are barely in the game at all. With a .250 batting average, a player struggles to remain in the sport as a professional. So the difference between super-stardom, millions of dollars, and massive contracts, and barely being in the business at all is half an at-bat out of ten. That's a mere 5 percent difference.

In Formula 1 motor racing, or F1, qualifying times are measured in thousandths of a second. The difference between first and third is often just tenths of a second, yet the advantage of being first, and sitting in the "pole position" is huge. It gives the driver a much better shot at finishing first and winning the race.

I have enjoyed watching bobsledding in the Winter Olympics for years. In the Olympics, the aim is to get the gold medal. Of course everybody wants to win gold, because who remembers who won the silver and the bronze? Most of the endorsements come with the gold medal. In the men's fours in bobsled recently, the difference between first – a gold medal, and fourth – no medal at all, was twelve one hundredths of a second. After years of practice, the endorsement difference for 0.12 seconds can be millions or tens of millions of dollars.

So, there are many examples of this in all aspects of life. It's not necessarily about being a hundred times better than the competition or even five or ten times better. When you understand the

Razor's Edge Reality, you'll see the significant advantage, and then there really is no competition. Here's another personal example: when I was selling real estate, I would make cold calls every day, five days a week from 8:30 in the morning until 10:00 a.m. However, after I implemented the Razor's Edge Theory, I started calling from 8:30 in the morning until 10:01 a.m., Monday to Friday.

You might wonder what an extra minute did for me. Well, in that extra minute, I'd be able to make two additional phone calls. I could make two calls in such a short space of time because I'd only phone them and say, "Hi, this is Tony Neumeyer with XYZ Realty. I'm calling to see if you, or someone you know, would be interested in buying or selling real estate in the next six months." If they said no, I would simply reply, "Thank you very much. I appreciate your time." I'd hang up and be on to the next person. It could be a very quick and unobtrusive call, but if they were interested, then we might get in to a bit of a discussion. During that hour and a half (plus a minute), I'd be able to make about one hundred calls.

Although that extra minute might not seem like much of a difference, I could make two calls in that time. Looking at that long-term, that meant ten extra calls per week, just in that one extra minute. Out of every ten calls I made, I'd find somebody who said they would have some interest in doing real estate business in the next six months or so. Now, did they all do something, and did they all do it with me? No, but that didn't matter. I was just looking for people who were interested in doing some business, so the extra ten phone calls, that extra one minute per day, gave me one extra prospect per week.

That's at least an extra fifty prospects per year. If just **one in ten** of those prospects did go on to do business with me, that would be tens of thousands of dollars in my pocket annually for that one extra minute per day. In fact, it worked. It worked amazingly well with just one single extra minute. I could've added an extra five minutes if I had wanted to, but I had other things going on, and I had already done ninety minutes of calling. Making two extra calls in that short period of time added about 2 percent more, a razor's edge. Making the time to do 2 percent more per day made all the difference, putting tens of thousands of extra dollars in my pocket each and every year.

Given that this managing of your time and journaling your daily experiences are so important, I am going to expand on those two thoughts with a little more detail. You will want to keep a journal as well as us a time planner, they are quite different and have different purposes as you will see.

Let's talk first about your time planner. Whether you use a computer-based time management system or you use a paper book system it isn't important. What is important is that you use a system to keep yourself on track and efficient. Remember that one minute can make you a lot of money. So here are a couple of key points. First, you want to plan each day prior to the start of the day. Starting your day knowing what you are going to do already makes a huge difference to your overall productivity. You do this by taking a few minutes at the end of your day and inputting the next day's to do list, in order of importance, and scheduling what you need to get done along with the time segments you need. Be sure to include travel and preparation time as well. Often when you don't have your tasks scheduled there is a tendency to do those items that are easy or simple, but not necessarily the most important.

By scheduling your day fully, you will largely avoid those time-wasters that you have undoubtedly discovered when you did the time-mapping exercise. Be sure to also schedule your personal time, your eating time, and the time with your family and so on. Doing this will empower you and your direction in life. This is not meant to eliminate spontaneity; just know that if your plan changes during your day that you are in control of that as well. You will be able to look at your calendar to decide if today is a day that you can be spontaneous and change your plans.

Using a time planner to keep you on track each day is different to keeping a journal. Keeping a journal, for our purposes, is the daily writing down of your accomplishments, your challenges, and other notes of significance to you. At the end of each week, you should review your journal and look carefully to see what you can learn from the week's activities and notes you've made. Additionally, make weekly notes about anything significant, and then review those notes on a monthly basis. You will want to review your goals, plans and tasks regularly; however, it is important that once a year (I like to do it the first few days of January) you sit down and review what you have accomplished in the past year and what you will accomplish in the coming year.

Careful notes and the review of these notes will help to keep you on track and assist you to create and refine your seven-minute PPM, which we will discuss in detail in just a couple more chapters. It's important for you to know where you're starting from so that you have a "yardstick" for measuring progress. You need to know how much is in your bank account, where you stand today, and the specifics of where you're going.

The notes you make in your journal don't always have to be 100 percent positive; that's life and sometimes things get in the way. If you fail to complete a task, make a note of that. Explain *why* you failed to complete it, and see if there's a way to avoid that issue in the future. Make a note of what you were doing that prevented you from completing your assigned task. Were you doing something unnecessary or at the bottom of your priority list just to get out of fulfilling the task, or was it something worthwhile that kept you from what you should have done that day? Maybe you were just looking for excuses. Analyzing your notes honestly can be insightful, can help you to improve, and can lead you to a point where fewer and fewer adjustments are required.

Create an early morning routine for yourself so you begin each day with a positive expectation. When you get up in the morning, what do you do first? And next? And then after that? By setting up a routine for yourself and sticking to it, you'll help drive home the process of getting through the tasks you set out for each day. In order to accomplish everything, you may find that you need to get up a little earlier in the morning, or stay up later in the evening. That's what worked best for me. When I first instituted this routine in my life, I decided I was going to get up an hour earlier each day so I could do what I wanted to accomplish. I started getting up at 5:00 a.m. instead of 6:00 a.m. It may have only been an hour, but that difference meant that I could start making phone calls to people at 8:00 a.m. in the Eastern Time zone. By changing one simple aspect of my usual routine, I built a multi-million-dollar business. This is a "Razor's Edge Reality" technique.

That precious time before the usual hustle and bustle of the day can be invaluable. Think what an extra hour a day could mean to you over time. We considered this in an earlier chapter when we discussed learning from a recording while driving. If you found that extra hour every day, you'd gain more than an additional 350 hours a year. Think what you could accomplish in that time.

A university class generally runs for forty-eight to sixty hours per semester, per course. So if you freed up 350 hours per year, you could complete approximately five university classes in that time. Okay, we're not talking about the homework in addition to that class time. Even if you only found half that much time, think how far ahead you could be a year or two, or three from now.

It all comes down to allocating your time and determining your priorities in advance. When you redefine your priorities, they need to be *absolute* priorities in your life; half-hearted priorities will not change your life. How you allocate your time is going to determine your productivity, your advancement, and potentially your success and future wealth throughout your life.

By now you have measured your time allocations by the 5 minute segments and figured out how much time you're actually wasting in a day. You should now know how much available time you have to start building toward your better and brighter future, simply by being more efficient with your time.

As you plan your time, check and make sure that each activity you're doing is taking you toward what you want to achieve so you know you're being as productive as you can possibly be. There's no time-wasting now, not if you want to progress. Don't cheat yourself of your time because we have only a finite period available to

147

us. Each of us has twenty-four hours in every single day. That's it: no more, no less. What you can produce in that period of time will ultimately make the difference in your life. So fill your time with whatever it takes to move you toward your goals and objectives.

Spend no more than about ninety minutes on any particular project without taking a small break. Get up and walk around the room, do some push-ups or chin-ups, or just do something active that gets the blood flowing in the brain. Activity helps to keep the mind creative and active. Taking breaks will ultimately keep you more productive. Place a timer on your desk and set it so you're assured of taking breaks. You're now learning how to become more efficient with your time. Set specific times to answer emails. This can be whenever you like, but it can be a huge time-waster so schedule the time one to three times a day depending on your job and the type of emails you receive.

Don't waste time on Facebook or other social media platforms. Use them to your advantage if and when you are starting your new business, but understand the difference. There are currently 1.1 billion users of Facebook, and on average they spend seventeen minutes per day on the site.[18] That's the *average*, and you know some spend much more time. Spending time purposefully is of course different, but be sure you use that time effectively and limit the time you spend there.

Typically, studies show that when people write down everything they're doing, they find that they're wasting about thirty to ninety minutes a day at work, or they can identify about the same daily amount of unproductive time within their daily routines.[19] I'm curious what *your* number is. How does all this relate to the Razor's Edge Reality?

As I have pointed out, you don't have to be that much better than the next person to go from mediocrity to massive wealth. By consistently doing a little bit more and standing out just a little more often, you can get there. Vince Lombardi, when he was coaching football, focused his players on what he called "The Second Effort" concept: Okay, they've got you by the legs, they're about to tackle you. Give it that extra push, get that extra yard, get that extra *two* yards, and occasionally, you will break the tackle and go *many* more yards, or go for a touchdown.

That's exactly the type of concept I am talking about: doing just a little bit more, doing a little extra, going that extra mile; that's the Razor's Edge Reality. As you develop your plan and picture your personal tasks and achievements in life, ask yourself, "What can I do just a little bit better? What can I do just a little bit more of?"

Another key to a successful future is to do **more of what works**. When you find something that is working for you, when you find something that is successfully moving you toward to your goals, do more of it to create more success. As you do, you will increase your speed toward all of your objectives. When marketers are testing a campaign, they test, test, and test again. But as they discover which parts of the campaign are working, they focus their energy and their budget allocation to capitalize on what they have already been able to prove is working. If you pay attention, it will become absolutely clear to you how every extra Razor's Edge effort increases the ease and speed with which you can achieve your goals. Utilize this technique in every area of your life.

You're going to do the work anyway, so why not spend just a little extra effort doing it well, and doing it in a way that will take you where you want to go? You might as well make the work as financially worthwhile as possible, and create the success you're after.

As you implement your Razor's Edge activities you will begin to realize that there's very little competition out there because your competition isn't doing this. They don't have the Razor's Edge Reality mindset. They don't understand how these realities work or even that they exist. They're just going about their days as best they can, and that's OK for them, but it's not OK for you! If it were, you wouldn't be reading this book! You and I both know that you want better, and you want more. What suits others doesn't suit you. For you to earn ten times more money than the competition, you don't have to be ten times better. You just need to do a little more; just be a few percentage points better.

Don't worry about the competition in your field; it isn't of any consequence. When accomplishing your goals, 80 percent of the task will be just showing up and completing the task. It's that next 20 percent that is going to really make the difference in your life. The truth is that, of the 20 percent of people who do show up, only 20 percent of those people are really purposely making "it" happen. Whatever your "it" is. It will be easy for you to become part of that 4 percent or less when you use the Razor's Edge techniques.

I was flying first-class recently and I glanced at the ten people around me filling the first-class seats. A couple of people were sleeping; four people working on their computers; two were reading what looked like something associated with business; two were doing just nothing; and then there was my wife and me. The majority of people around me weren't just having leisure time on that first-class flight; they were making good use of the time, as was I. They were working on getting ahead. You too can use these kinds of times to be productive. Sometimes productive means resting, but if you're stuck on a long-haul flight, put the time to good use. You could listen to music you've wanted to catch up on, or you could listen to an audiobook or a recording of an inspirational speaker.

Whatever You Do, Do It On Purpose

When you learn to use your time as productively as you possibly can, that's when you really start to get ahead. Remember, time is finite; when it becomes available to you, make the best of it. If you are sitting in a waiting room, do some reading from your smartphone or listen to an audiobook. Begin to see these moments as opportunities to move your life ahead, and take them, don't lose them. To be sure you can take advantage of them, have something with you that you can listen to or read when these times occur unexpectedly.

Plan for this kind of extra time and implement that plan when time appears so you can take advantage of it. Don't waste that time! Are there phone calls you can make? Could you make some notes in your journal? Is there some reading you could do that would help you move forward?

Don't Let Your Downtime Plan You

Follow Jim Rohn's words and be sure that you're taking those simple disciplines and moving yourself closer to your preferred reality every day, as much as possible throughout the day.

As we move toward the end of the book, we're going to bring all of the aspects we've discussed together to create your inspirational seven-minute PPM that's going to change your life. By now you should have taken your list of goals and added the dates when you want to have each of them completed (see chapter seven exercise). If you haven't done it yet, be sure you do that now. You'll need those specific goals when you create your PPM.

Be clear on when you want each of the items on that list to occur. Set goals for each of the time frames: six months, one year, two years, five years, and seven years. For the purpose of this exercise, we won't be going past seven years, but I encourage you to have a vision and plan for ten years down the road and beyond. For now, focus on generating a list that clearly states what you want and when you want it.

A man's mind is stretched by a new idea or

sensation, and never shrinks back to its former

dimensions.

Oliver Wendell Holmes Sr.

NINE

BUILD YOUR BRAIN MUSCLE

In chapter eight, we talked about the Razor's Edge Reality, and I hope you appreciated how by doing just a little bit more, you can create significant rewards and huge changes in your life. If a rocket ship is on its way to the moon and at the beginning misses its course by just a degree or two, it could miss the moon by thousands of miles – but that's a negative manifestation. When you look at that same equation in a positive way, just a little change can make a massive difference down the road.

To carry on from there, it's important to understand and exercise your brain muscle. Of course, the brain is not a muscle in the traditional sense, and we can't exercise it in the same way we do the rest of the muscles in our bodies. However, we can still exercise it; in fact, it's the most powerful organ in our entire body. Your brain has the ability to change how you feel, how you look, your mood, your financial well-being, and every other aspect of your being.

To gain the maximum benefits in brain exercise, you want your brain to be able to develop and create images. The more vivid and real those images are, the more, and more rapidly, you will be able to create them. Nothing is created physically without first starting as a mental picture. For example, the high-rise in the downtown area of the city wasn't built without plans, but before those plans were even drawn, somebody had to visualize what would be laid out within them.

Building your brain muscle can be done anywhere, any time. Whenever you have a moment of downtime during the day, you can do it. Imagine you're standing in line at your local coffee shop. While waiting to be served, you can start to visualize something. It can be something you want to create, or just something in general, but I suggest visualizing something concrete that you really do want to create.

The more powerfully that you create these images, and the more emotion you create with your images, the more powerful they become to your subconscious, making it easier for your subconscious to act on them and help manifest them. By doing these exercises in your spare time or downtime, you're using all your time positively, in a way that's going to help improve your life. You can choose to do nothing at all in your downtime, but a neutral course of action will likely not move you forward. And as you'll recall, if you're not moving forward, you're moving backward.

If you struggled at all with the visualization of the tomato, then take a look at this simple visualization exercise. You will quickly discover a number of benefits.

CHAPTER NINE, EXERCISE ONE

Visualization employs the right half of your brain. The right hemisphere of the brain is the place for experimentation, metaphoric thinking, playfulness, flexibility, curiosity, synergy, artistry, synthesizing, solution finding, and general risk-taking. The right hemisphere is the center of your capability to visualize things.[20]

The following simple exercise will enhance your ability to have clear mental pictures. As with anything else in life, with a little daily practice the creation of clear mental images will quickly become almost second nature to you. About 60 to 65 percent of us automatically think in images even though we may not be aware of it.[21] This exercise will help your brain to focus on images you want to see, rather than those that automatically appear. Although the exercise is fairly simple, it is extremely powerful and designed to help you practice deep concentration with focus. Used consistently, it will also help to improve your brain's ability to retain visual imagery and begin to program your subconscious.

- To start with, draw a on a piece of paper a standard geometric shape, colored in a primary shade: a blue square, a red circle, or a yellow rectangle, for example. Just use whatever springs to mind. The drawn image will assist your brain in keeping the picture fresh and clear.

- Concentrate your mind, and focus on the shape you've drawn; then close your eyes and mentally picture the shape. Don't worry if you don't get a clear image to begin with. The purpose of trying another visualization exercise is to build new circuits, or neural pathways, in your brain. We want to get your brain firing on all cylinders, just as you would exercise any other muscle. Start off with simple images and eventually you'll be able to visualize more in-depth images, ideas of greater complexity.

- Now stare at the image for around thirty seconds, then close your eyes again, and "see" it in your mind again. This time see if you can keep that mental image strong for thirty seconds. Keep practicing until you can hold a strong mental image. Although you might not see the image clearly at the beginning, you are developing a deep state of concentration. Like anything, practice it, and you will get better at it.

- Next, imagine a more vivid image. Imagine it becoming energized and alive. Imagine you're tracing the outline with your finger, and brightly-colored light appears from the end of your finger, making the edges of the shape shine and spark. Then watch that spark as it fills the image from the outside in. Keep imagining your finger going repeatedly around the edge of the shape until you don't need your finger to see the light tracing around the outside.

Again, as you practice this, it will become easier.

Another benefit of this exercise is that you will be actively using your imagination to create mental pictures. This process will help you in other ways as well. It is a form of practicing to be creative, meaning that it will help an idea flow as you move into the creation of free-flowing ideas, talked about a little later in the chapter. You may also discover that it gives you a feeling of well-being and has the benefit of lifting your mood too.

Once you've mastered this basic visualization exercise, you can progress to creating a mental movie in which you are the star! You'll be able to imagine yourself reaching your goals, whether they are in business or your personal life. In fact, why not go for both? These techniques are also helpful if you would like to eliminate bad habits or give something up, such as smoking. These can all be part of your seven-minute PPM. You will be using positive language when you do this. In that respect, you won't be "giving something up" (which implies negativity and loss), you will be choosing to gain something, such as good health or weight loss. We'll touch more on that in the next chapter. If you use your visualizations effectively, you can do something that helps improve you and moves you toward your objectives and goals much faster.

CHAPTER NINE, EXERCISE TWO

Create a picture in your mind of a place you've been that you absolutely loved. This is slightly more advanced than visualizing a geometric shape. Wherever it is, picture that spot in your mind right now, and hold on to it for the next fifteen seconds. See if you can bring back that feeling you had there, and concentrate on how enjoyable and positive it was when you were last there. You can actually start to manifest things in the future by thinking about them today.

Napoleon Hill, in *Think and Grow Rich*, says, "You will become whatever you think about most often." That's largely true, with *some* limitations, but the things we consciously focus on the most will start to manifest in our lives. You can use this process for many areas of your life.

Your thoughts and visions will start to change your life both quickly and over time. All of this will start with just a few minutes a day. If, in the last exercise, you were able to picture that wonderful spot you enjoyed so much, then you're well on your way to creating whatever you want in your future. If picturing your place posed a bit of a challenge, don't worry; you will become more practiced and proficient at it.

You're going to become very good at this; it isn't really that difficult once you get the hang of it. Here's another example of creating things in your life: when I was young I used to tell my mom that I thought eating was a waste of time. Taking all the time to prepare a meal then sitting down at the table to eat seemed like a waste of valuable time. I wondered why we couldn't just take some pills that gave us all the nutrition and energy we needed. We could stop wasting time eating and just be out doing whatever we wanted again.

It's funny how we create things in our minds and in our future; later, one of the businesses that I created, and made a great deal of money at, was a vitamin business. I took many of those great supplements myself (I still take them today), and they are virtually meals in capsule form. I thought about that from a very young age, and it wasn't until several years later that I started to actually manifest the idea in reality.

I'm talking about becoming a professional image maker. People use their minds in many different ways, and the truth is that most don't use them in the most powerful ways they possibly could. They don't create their pictures *or* create their futures. So how do you get better at creating those pictures in your mind? It's simple: practice.

One of the keys when you start to create pictures in your mind is to see yourself in possession of what you desire. Picture yourself in that new car, in that new home, enjoying the new lifestyle, enjoying the travel. Picture it so clearly that you can actually feel yourself in those positions; feel the warmth of the sun on your cruise, or whatever your ideal image is. As you become more proficient at doing that, you'll find that you're able to achieve your goals and objectives more quickly and overcome doubt. This is important because doubts become black holes that can draw you in and suck away all of your dreams. Using your PPM will help remove doubt from your thought patterns. That's not to say that doubt won't occasionally creep in, but as you create concise pictures of your future and your life as you move forward, you will be able to beat out doubt. Instead, you'll be able to continue to create what it is that you picture in your mind.

What you see is what you get. So the more vivid and emotional you can make these pictures in your mind, the more likely it is you'll be able to manifest them in reality. Gaining new knowledge, as we've discussed, will help you grow and work toward what you're trying to accomplish in your life. And remember, you want to become an ideas person. You want ideas to start flowing into your brain all the time.

IT TAKES ONLY ONE NEW IDEA TO CHANGE YOUR LIFE

Once you are able to create pictures in your mind at will, you will also want ideas to be flowing on a regular basis. Think of some of the crazy ideas that have gone on to become businesses worth millions or billions of dollars. It may have all started with an App or some other new technology. There are many different ideas that might occur to you, but you must be open to allowing them to flow through your brain and to putting them down on paper so that you can potentially research them and utilize them.

This is something else you should do in your journal each day: come up with ideas and write them down as they occur to you. If you don't have time to write them down immediately, you could record them on your (smart)phone so you can write them in your journal later. You might even keep a separate section in your journal where you practice this brainstorming. Sit for five, ten, or twenty minutes, and just put down ideas. Remember, when you're brainstorming, it doesn't matter if the ideas are bad, good, or absolutely awful. Right now, the point is to just get ideas flowing because if you're going to get ahead in life, you're going to need some ideas about how you're going to do that. While you're brainstorming, create a picture in your mind of what your perfect relationship looks like. Write down your ideas, your thoughts, and descriptions of the pictures that you're creating in your mind. This is all part of building your brain muscle.

CHAPTER NINE, EXERCISE THREE

For this exercise, you'll need to return to all the goals and objectives that you've put down on paper so far.

- Go through the lists you've made, and visualize each and every one of them. Take as long as you need. By now I expect you can call on your visualization techniques almost at will. If you're still having a little difficulty, go back and start again with the simple geometric shape.

- Visualize each of your goals in-depth and with as much detail as you possibly can. See if they evoke any emotion within you. Make a note of any goals that evoke the strongest emotions. You may want to focus on these ones first.

- Next, gather physical photos, either actual photo-graphs or images taken from magazines or online, that represent places you want to go or things you want to have. These could be illustrations, pictures from online, brochures, or anything really. Have fun with it. There's no pressure, but you want to do this so you will have a visual conception of each of the goals you plan to achieve. I want you to have this both in your mind and in a tangible form. The reason why this is important will all become clear in chapter ten when you create your seven-minute PPM.

Next, think about the following questions:

- Are you going to start a business?
- Have you thought about this as one of your ways of getting ahead?
- If so, what type of business?
- Do you have enough money to do that now?
- Or do you need money to get started?
- What kind of business would it be?

If you're trying to move to the next level in your career, or create a new career for yourself, it's a good idea to take the time to really think about what you're interested in, what you've already accomplished in your life, and what your particular strengths are. Very often though, we ruminate alone. What if you were to ask others for their input? What would someone else say you're good at? Has a friend, co-worker or former boss mentioned to you that they felt you were particularly good at something? Most of us are really surprised to hear about the things other people see in us. While I understand that someone else's perceptions of you may not align with your own self-image, it can be valuable information that should not be dismissed simply because you may not agree with it. Rather than ignoring these insights from other people, you should explore them with the idea of improving wherever possible. Doing so may help you to refine and refocus your thoughts on a future business or career plan.

If you do talk with someone else about your plans, be sure it's someone who has some experience in business and who is likely to support your ideas, not tear them down. Asking someone you don't completely trust, on occasion, may result in a negative experience. This can be part of your brainstorming session, your idea gathering, and your brain-building exercises. That said, if you ask someone who has experience and they have reservations about your idea, take heed. I have seen some pretty lame ideas on television, in business magazines and at opportunity events. People have spent fortunes when there was simply no market so research the market for your idea thoroughly.

GIVE YOURSELF A REWARD!

As you move forward toward attaining your goals, it's also important to recognize certain accomplishments. Reward yourself with something meaningful, even if it's just something small. You'll have to figure out what a reward is for you. It might be a nice dinner out or a holiday. It might be as simple as a walk around the park, but make sure it's something that will allow you to revel in the accomplishments you'll make along your path to success.

Along the way, remember that you may have some setbacks. You may have some small failures, even, but that's OK because you're going to write them down in your journal, and you're going to learn from them. I too have had many of these learning moments in my life, and continue to do so, to this day. You actually *want* to have those learning moments because if you're not falling down, you're not pushing hard enough to learn. Setbacks show you that you're gaining ground and moving ahead.

We've already talked, in chapter four, about making a decision and being absolute in that decision. Without an absolute decision, there is no decision at all. It's time to decide that you're going to do this. You can't just *try* to do it. I often use the following example when teaching groups of people. I'll bring someone up to the front of the room and ask them to sit on a chair. Then I ask them to "try to stand up." They stand up. "Hold on, no, no, you just stood up," I say. I make them sit back down and say again, "OK, I'd like you to try to stand up." They stand up again and I say, "No, no, no, hold on. You just made a decision and you stood up. What I'd like you to do is *try* to stand up." After two or three cycles like this, the point usually becomes clear: they can't *try* to stand up. They either stand up or they don't, period. They've either made the decision to stand up or made the decision to remain seated, but when we use the word "try," our brains get confused because it's not an *absolute* direction. When we say, "try to stand up," our brain moves us straight to the goal because we're used to standing up. We've pictured it and done it thousands of times in the past. Our brains automatically assume that if we *try* to stand up, we actually *want* to stand up. The brain moves us directly to that point. Realize that *trying* is not an acceptable effort because it actually confuses the brain. Trying will set you back. In fact, it might be a good idea to remove this word from your vocabulary.

According to Lou Tice, the founder of the Pacific Institute, the reticular activating system in our brains is actually a filter that sifts through the noise around us and shields us from great anxiety. It also assists us in filtering images, sounds, and distractions that could be life-threatening if we allowed them to distract us when we should be concentrating on something else, such as driving a car or walking down the street. The same is true when we're setting goals. Of course your objective is to set only positive goals, but sometimes, if you're not careful, you can be bombarded with negativity, and suddenly your brain will start moving you down that negative path. We've already discussed how we are constantly bombarded with messages or brain noise such as ads on television and the radio.

You must continually provide your subconscious mind with positive direction to allow it to manifest in your life in a positive way. Keep in mind that the reticular activating system can also filter out the positive. However, using the techniques we've covered so far in addition to your PPM, you'll find that you'll be able to change your brain, directly influencing it to move in the direction you want, which in turn will allow your brain to create everything you want.

Be sure not to think small because small challenges may not challenge you at all. I want you to think big. Think outside of your comfort zone. Have you ever thought about earning as much money in a month as you do right now in a year? Is the thought too much for you? For a lot of people, thinking about something that big is too much of a stretch and, in fact, becomes so daunting that they start to shut down. You will need to make your goals attainable and realistic, of course, but I think it's possible for most people to visualize what it would be like to earn as much money in a month as they currently do in a year.

Let's take it a step further. What would it be like to earn in a week as much as you currently earn in a year? Does that throw your brain into overload? It's OK either way. It's just a question, something I'm throwing out there for you to think about. When I started earning as much in a month as many executives earn in a year, it was something I found very, very exciting.

Suddenly I had lots of money left over at the end of the month, whereas in the past, after my bankruptcy, I'd always had too much month left at the end of my money! It is exciting and fun to have that much cash flow. Initially though, as much as I had thought it would be great to be earning six figures a month, it was one of those things I couldn't fully comprehend, even though I knew I wanted it. However, when I started making tens of thousands per month, I was then able to understand what it might be like to make six figures or more per month, and what that would do to my life.

As you start to progress and as you start to grow into your comfort zone, you'll find that your comfort zone expands, and so does your outlook and your ability to achieve more. But don't worry about where you are today; where you are today is where you are today. It's not where you will be a year from now, or two years, or five years.

Eventually you're going to completely understand and internalize this material and these techniques. That said, until you know it inside and out, until it becomes your habitual routine, you're going to need a little discipline. So, be like a salesperson, practicing your material, and rehearsing your presentations.

As you become an idea generator and an expert at visualization, you'll find that your life will start to manifest itself the way that you're dreaming it. For me this happened quite quickly. The changes started to manifest themselves within days and weeks of implementing the strategies in this book. This brain we have is probably the world's finest computer. You have the conscious brain that will come up with the ideas of what you want in your life. These ideas will help you understand where you'd like to be. However, it is the subconscious brain that actually manifests those thoughts and moves us forward toward them.

We're about to get into the process of programming your computer, your brain, your subconscious, so that you can build your life in whatever way you choose. You're going to use your conscious brain to build the ideas, to build the plan, and then you're going to let the subconscious manifest that plan. The subconscious brain is going to strategize while you do the physical work, and your continual programming of your subconscious mind is what will get you where you want to be.

As you put this into practice and get better at it, you're going to find that more and better ideas will come to you, and they'll also become more free-flowing. You'll have many ideas about ways to manifest the life that you want for yourself. As you exercise more, gather pictures of the things you want in your life, and then start to imagine them in your conscious mind, you'll become better and better at manifesting those things through your subconscious abilities.

In the next chapter, we'll bring it all together. I am really excited about the next chapter because this is what we've been working toward all along, creating your seven-minute PPM (Personal Programming Message). Be sure, before you move on to the next chapter, that you've completed all the exercises from this and the previous chapters. Unless you've completed all the exercises to this point, you won't be able to complete your seven-minute PPM.

Thoughts become things.

If you see it in your mind,

you will hold it in your hand.

Bob Proctor

TEN

YOUR SEVEN MINUTES – THE MASTER KEY

In the last chapter we talked about teaching your brain to become more powerful in its ability to create ideas and vivid images that your subconscious mind can produce. Throughout this book, you've completed a variety of exercises and I have been talking about the seven-minute PPM (Personal Programming Message) that you'll create for yourself. This is the most powerful exercise in the book, one that will manifest and program your subconscious mind to attract everything you are after into your life in ways you are not even aware of at this moment.

We already know that it's you who will initially generate your thoughts in your conscious mind, and that your subconscious mind will then act on them to manifest them. The subconscious part of your brain doesn't have the ability to judge the positive or negative direction you create. It only acts upon the thoughts and influences of the conscious mind. I have also explained that our expectations become realities. Our subconscious moves us toward our expectations, and we can build our expectations and even our ability to expect what we want to happen in our lives using our PPMs. We also know that what you believe to be true for you is, in fact, true. And where you are today doesn't have any weight as to where you can be tomorrow, two months from now, or two years from now.

Your Personal Programming Message is really the master key to everything that you've learned and worked on to this point. So what exactly is this seven-minute PPM, and what's it all about? Your Personal Programming Message is a seven-minute audio recording of your own voice that is going to change and program your subconscious to help you achieve whatever it is that you choose to achieve. When your subconscious hears your own voice, it opens and responds more rapidly because it recognizes you. Having someone else record a message may work for you, but it won't be as effective as if it is in your own voice.

Keeping in mind that all goals need to be realistic, attainable, and exact, remember too that they need a timeframe associated with them. For example, if you're talking about sales, be specific not only about the number of sales that you want to make, but also the timeframe in which you want to make them: a year, a month, a week. Similarly, if you have a weight loss goal, set your target weight, or your target weight loss. An example for a real estate salesperson might sound like this: "I make a minimum of one sale per week. I do this by enthusiastically making cold calls from 8:30 a.m. until 10:01 a.m., Monday through Friday, employing the Razor's Edge Reality in all aspects of what I do. I also contact a minimum of 10,000 people each quarter via my direct mail (or email) marketing campaigns." You can see what I mean and expand on the specific tasks it would take to accomplish this particular goal.

Goal setting is crucial to getting what you want in your life. I cannot tell you enough times that in order to achieve goals, you need to have a clear idea in your mind of what those goals are. Wishy-washy just doesn't cut it here. Goal setting is used in business as a powerful way to motivate personnel, and here you will use it to motivate and, more importantly, inspire yourself.

The value of goal setting is so universally recognized that goal-setting basics are incorporated in many company policies. It's also accepted as one of the most useful and compelling inspirational practices in human resource management, and it's often used for organizational behavior practices. Many of you will already be familiar with the idea of setting SMART goals:

Specific

Measurable

Attainable

Relevant

Time-bound

Keep those adjectives firmly in your mind when you are setting your own goals, and you will be on your way to accomplishing them.

In the late 1960s, Dr. Edwin Locke laid the groundwork in goal-setting and motivation research. In his 1968 article, "Toward a Theory of Task Motivation and Incentives," he stated that, "employees were motivated by clear goals and appropriate feedback." Locke went on to say, "Working toward a goal provided a major source of motivation to actually reach the goal – which, in turn, improved performance." I know I have found this to be true in my own case: when I set a goal for myself, I measure my progress and make sure I am on track and moving toward attaining it.

Forty years later, we probably don't recognize how revolutionary this statement was at the time. Let's take a look at what else Locke told us about goal setting, and find ways we can apply his theories to our goals.

GOAL SETTING THEORY

Locke's research clearly demonstrated that there is a relationship between the difficulty of a goal, how well defined that goal is, and how a person will perform a task. The more specific and difficult a goal is, the better the performance of a task will be. This is also why it is very important to fully define your tasks. Vague or easy goals will not yield as strong a result. When I said, "think big," this is what I was referring to. A goal that is too small will be dismissed as unworthy by your subconscious.

Positive and current language also comes into play here. If you tell someone to "try hard" or "try to do your best," it will not be effective. Remember the brain can't move you toward "trying;" it either does it or it doesn't. Using positive language in present tense allows your brain to picture you in possession of the goal. As such, it will move you toward that vision. Grow your comfort zone! Your goals should stretch you and help you develop as a person. They must be attainable, but they should also be worthy of the stretch.

After Locke published his ground-breaking article, Dr. Gary Latham, another researcher, went on to study the effects of goal setting in the workplace. His results supported what Locke had already found, so an inseparable link was formed between the importance of goal setting and its reflection on workplace performance.

In 1990, Locke and Latham co-published the influential work, *A Theory of Goal Setting and Task Performance*. This book looked at the importance of setting specific and difficult goals, plus three other important characteristics of potentially profitable goal setting.

THE FIVE IMPORTANT PRINCIPLES OF GOAL SETTING

In order to motivate anyone, and in particular you, your goals must have the following attributes:

- Clarity
- Challenge
- Commitment
- Feedback
- Task complexity

Let's look at each of those points in turn.

Clarity

As already mentioned, clear goals are measurable and explicit. When a goal is set clearly, it has a definite timeframe for completion, and there is no room for misunderstanding in your subconscious. You know what's expected of you, and the result is your source of motivation. When a goal is vague or general, as in the phrase, "take some initiative," it has no inspirational value because the reward for the behavior is not clear and fixed. Clear goals use specific and measurable markers.

Remembering the SMART acronym: ensure the clarity of your goals by making them **S**pecific, **M**easurable, **A**ttainable, **R**elevant and **T**ime-bound. It's a must for your subconscious.

Challenge

Another important aspect to bear in mind when goal setting, is the level of challenge you are setting for yourself. When you know that what you set out to accomplish will be well received, you'll discover a natural, innate inspiration to do a good job of things, not only for yourself but also to benefit your family. As your goals increase in difficulty, the rewards increase exponentially. If you know that you're going to be well compensated for achieving your goals, your enthusiasm will be naturally boosted, as will your drive to get it done, and get it done well. When setting goals, assign each a degree of challenge. If an assignment is too easy, you probably will not exert much in the way of effort.

However, it is important that you strike a balance between setting challenging goals and those that are realistic. Remember that it is possible to become de-motivated or uninspired, particularly if you set a goal that is impossible to achieve. We all have a strong need for success and achievement and are therefore more inspired by challenging but realistic and attainable goals. Remember the **A** in SMART goals, and set goals that are achievable and **A**ttainable.

Commitment

For goals to be effective, we need to understand them consciously and subconsciously. All of us are more likely to "buy in" to a goal when we feel we've been part of creating and setting that goal. Your commitment to attaining your goals and the level of difficulty of those goals will often work together. It's common sense really, but the harder the goal is, the more commitment is required to attain it. When goals are easy, not a lot of motivation, inspiration, or will is needed to complete them. The subconscious sees easy goals as not requiring its effort. If you work on something difficult, you will probably come across challenges requiring more inspiration, discipline and incentive. Your brain recognizes this as a challenge it must help you with and that is also where your PPM comes in – it will help you feel that you want to stay committed so you do in fact, stay committed.

Feedback

In addition to choosing the right kinds of goals, for your goal-setting program to be effective you need to include feedback. Feedback presents you with an opportunity to clarify your expectations and to consider adjusting the difficulty of your goals. It also allows you to recognize your progress. Setting interim targets allows you to determine for yourself how you're doing. You should use these regular sessions to measure specific progress along the way. We'll discuss this in more detail shortly, that is, the idea of breaking things down into small, manageable tasks. Interim targets are especially important if your ultimate goals are going to take you a considerable amount of time to reach.

Remember, your SMART goals need to be **M**easurable, which means that clear progress can be seen. If you're unsure where to get this feedback, perhaps a mentor or someone on a similar journey can provide unbiased feedback. Taking the time to sit down with some-one else and discuss your goal performance can be very helpful for your long-term improvement, but it is not essential.

When I was in real estate, I would graph my sales and dollar earn-ings with each sale. This would give me instant feedback and for me was a real motivator. I strived to reach the top of the graph and exceed it. Using my PPM, I was able to do that. In fact the year I began using my PPM I doubled the number of sales and earnings. It was a great feeling!

Task Complexity

The last important part of your goal setting introduces two addi-tional requirements for success. For goals that may be highly com-plex to attain, pay special attention to be sure they don't become too overwhelming. Chances are that you already have high levels of motivation and inspiration to better your life. However, you should not push yourself too hard without allowing for the complexity of the task. Think about this:

Give yourself adequate time to reach the goal or interim target.

Allow enough time to practice or learn what's required to attain success. This is why you will include the tasks you will use on the way to your goals in your seven-minute PPM.

This augments the **A**ttainable factor in SMART. The whole point of setting goals and targets is to facilitate your success, so don't allow conditions surrounding your goals to frustrate or inhibit you from accomplishing your objectives.

HOW TO WRITE YOUR
PERSONAL PROGRAMMING MESSAGE

Now we're going to break down each goal into the specific tasks you're going to do to attain that goal. You will include these tasks in your PPM. Start with the big goal. Let's say one of your goals is to earn $100,000 in the next year, and you are in sales. How many sales will it take to make that amount of money? How many presentations does it take to make a sale? How many prospects do you have to talk with in order to get a presentation? How many contacts or calls do you have to make to get a prospect?

Assuming it takes fifty sales to earn your $100,000 goal, what will your Personal Programming Message look like? It may go something like this: "I make a minimum of fifty sales in 2014 and every year. That is a minimum of one sale per week. I do this enthusiastically by making two professional presentations per week and by making a minimum of one hundred cold calls each week." And so on. Start with the larger picture and then break it down into tasks. Talk about and describe specifically all of the tasks that you're going use to accomplish the goals you have in mind, one at a time. Speak as you normally do, and choose words that will evoke strong emotion.

The ten most powerful keywords in advertising are considered to be *new, save, safety* (or *safe*), *proven, love, discover, guarantee, health, results*, and *you*. There are a couple of missing words, *free* and *sex*, but those have been overused. I give you this list of words because they are meant to evoke emotion in the reader, listener, or watcher of the ad. These are some keywords that are often used in advertising, and they're not meant to be the core of your PPM. Maybe some will work for you and you will want to use a few of these words when talking about your personal relationships or other goals. As I said, you will have your own vocabulary and words that having meaning to you.

Look for ways to create emotion in whatever you put together for your PPM. This is extremely important. When talking about relationships, it's also important to understand that you cannot change anyone else. Your goals and tasks must be for you and you alone. You can only change you. You can't change your partner, and you can't change the people around you. For these reasons, in focusing on a relationship goal, you want to be sure that you're keeping it very positive and only about you or the kind of person you will be, or the type person you want to attract. You can and should describe specifically the person you will and want to attract, but you cannot make an action of theirs a goal for you.

It's also very important to write in the present tense. When talking about the number of sales per week, say "I *make* a minimum of one sale per week," and state the year or timeframe specifically. You can use the current year, or you can say "*by* December 31, 20XX." For more examples of goals written for a PPM, see the Appendix at the end of this book.

There is a reason that we state not only the *goals* but also the *activities and tasks* associated with those goals. You want to program your mind to do these tasks enthusiastically and with the understanding and knowledge that they are part and parcel of attaining your goals. Just stating the end result is not enough, but when you create your PPM this way, you will find you actually get far more enjoyment out of the process of achieving your goals.

As for replacing your current beliefs with new and fresh beliefs, those old beliefs will remain in your subconscious mind until you replace them with the new ones. The longer your beliefs have been in place, the longer it'll take to reprogram the subconscious. Typically it takes twenty-one days to change any habit. So if you are new at this, as I expect you are, expect at least three weeks before you see results. However, you will probably start feeling enthusiastic about the process right away, and this will help carry you through those three weeks and beyond.

If a habit has been fully ingrained for many years, and has never been worked on at all, it may take a little longer. It might take at least thirty days to change a habit if you're building a new belief system – sometimes longer – but don't give up, keep reprogramming your subconscious. You're giving your subconscious something brand new to focus on and work through. This is not a one-time thing – three weeks and you are done. You must continue with your PPM as long as you want to continue to attain and maintain new goals. In other words, forever.

Previously your subconscious may have only worked on negative ideas or what randomly entered it through the outside messages delivered to you daily. You may not have worked much on moving toward the positive. As you add new beliefs to your belief system, you're going to be able to add more and more, bigger and greater beliefs and goals, and you're going to be able to accomplish more.

You must always use the positive form of a goal. In other words, phrase it in positive terminology. Never use negative words like don't, or *try*.

Think of a baseball pitching coach who doesn't understand that concept. He goes to the mound to talk with his pitcher and says, "OK, don't throw the ball over the plate to this batter. He's hitting over .300, and he's really on a hot streak, so just don't throw anything over the plate." The pitching coach walks back to the dugout. The pitcher winds up, lets the ball go, and what does he do? He throws it right over the middle of the plate, as he was told not to do. The batter hits it out of the park – home run! The pitcher gets in a lot of trouble from the pitching coach when, in fact, the pitching coach's instruction was wrong. The pitching coach shouldn't have said, "Don't throw it over the plate." Instead he should have said, "Be sure you throw the ball off the plate." In other words, he should have given the same instruction, but in a positive, rather than a negative manner.

The subconscious reacts strangely to negatives. A negative word is a "confuser" for the brain; instead, it reacts to the positive instruction, in the above case, "over the plate." When you're selecting your words and your story for yourself, put everything in the present tense, which is a positive instruction: "I make a minimum of one sale per week." You're making that sale in the present tense right now. The other thing you may have noticed is the word "minimum." When you use this word in the appropriate places it removes any limitations from your goals, allowing you to make or do more.

Your text needs to be direct, to the point, and simplistic. Your PPM is not meant to be a literary prizewinner. This is something to program your brain in a simple, straightforward, and fully descriptive manner that creates emotion. Think of and use words that create emotion for you, that have meaning for you, and that compel you to move toward your accomplishments. And be as detailed as you can.

Give yourself a solid description of the picture and goal you are going to manifest. Remember, you're painting a picture for your mind, and you're going to be listening to this seven-minute PPM twice a day, every day; once in the morning and once at night. You might want to talk to yourself in a detailed fashion that will paint and create the picture you desire.

Speak of yourself in the first person (I) in your PPM. Some people will tell you to use the second person (you), which I am told works, but I personally have always used first person, and I have found it to be 100 percent successful. Others I've worked with do the same, and they find it works perfectly also. Speak as though you're telling someone about yourself. Remember, use "I", not "you."

CREATING YOUR MESSAGE

Take your sets of goals and tasks in the different areas of your life – your finance, your business, your relationship, your fitness and health goals – and write these out in long form, breaking them down (as in the examples I have given you in Appendix A). Once you have done that, time yourself reading what you have written. You want to have a message that's approximately seven minutes. If it's five minutes, that's fine; if it's eight minutes, that's fine too. The point is for it to be short enough that you're not going to make excuses to avoid listening to it – every day, twice a day. If your PPM is seven minutes twice a day, that's just fourteen minutes out of your day, and you probably already found that much more time in your day after doing your time mapping exercise. Once you're satisfied with your message, you are going to record it so you can listen to it.

When you make your recording, I suggest you use a microphone. It's not necessary, but it is helpful. Make sure that the tone of your voice is calm, soothing, and natural. You want it to sound like your voice. Use a nice mellow tone of voice, but nothing too dramatic – you're not trying to create emotion with your voice. You will create the emotion internally because of the words you choose, not the tone you use. Remember that you will also be listening to this before you go to sleep, or even during your sleep if you choose to take that route.

Again, your voice isn't meant to create the emotion; your words and pictures are. If you're proficient with a computer you may decide that you want to add pictures to your PPM. You can create a video or a PowerPoint presentation with the sound of your voice narrating it. You can use the pictures you were gathering in the exercise in chapter nine. If you're a visual person, pictures along with the words can really benefit your emotional bond to the goals you're striving to achieve. This is definitely not necessary, and be sure not to use this method as an excuse for not creating your recording. Create your recording first, start using it, and add pictures later if you decide it will help you. Images can be beneficial because you are now using both your visual and auditory senses – you actually have a picture in front of you so your visualization may be easier. The key is to be in a relaxed state. If you create a video, just sit back, listen, and watch it. In both cases, to really train your subconscious, you still visualize what your words are saying.

No fake enthusiasm, just audio words (and pictures) that create emotion for you. You will likely find that the results begin immediately (this is often the case) but if it takes a bit of time, don't worry. As I said, it takes twenty-one days just to form a new habit, and if your habits have been ingrained for a considerable period of time, it may take even longer.

Listen to the recording you've made first thing in the morning as soon as you get out of bed, before you do virtually anything else. Maybe you take your bathroom break first, sure, but after that, while your brain is still open and nothing too much is flowing through it, sit down and plug your headphones into your Smartphone, computer, or whatever recording device you've used. Put yourself in a relaxed state, taking a few deep breaths if necessary to help with relaxation, and then turn on the recording. Listen to it carefully, and as you hear yourself state your goals and recite the tasks you've set out for yourself, make sure that you mentally visualize everything that you've laid out, as it's being said, each and every time you listen to your PPM. You want to fully internalize and visualize everything that you are hearing in your own voice.

Do this again last thing at night, just before you go to bed. Make it the last thing you do before you turn out the lights and go to bed, when your subconscious mind is receptive and open. Set yourself up in a relaxed state, take those seven minutes, and just listen to your own words, in your own voice. Don't worry if your voice sounds odd to you. Everybody feels that way at first. Just listen, and visualize your goals in that relaxed state. Afterward when you go to sleep, your subconscious mind will be working, formulating ways that it can manifest all you want to create in your life. You may find it easier to concentrate if you use a headset or earphones. It's not necessary, but headphones give you a little privacy and intimacy with your own voice.

So get into your relaxed state, listen to it first thing in the morning, last thing at night, and you'll find that you'll be *on-task* throughout your day and working toward your goals. You'll be able to achieve the objectives you set out to achieve.

This is actually a form of what is known as "subliminal learning," which refers to sending a message directly to your subconscious mind below the threshold of your conscious awareness. Subliminal messaging is possibly one of the most underrated and misunderstood performance-enhancing tools of recent times. The term "subliminal" comes from two Latin words, *sub*, meaning "under," and *limen*, meaning "threshold."

Subliminal programming is used to place ideas or thoughts into your subconscious mind, reinforcing information already stored in there and, in this case, that which you created. It can also increase your selective attention. Subliminal message reception is different to responding without any awareness. Subliminal messages involve you reacting to stimuli above your physiological threshold, but also below your perceptual threshold.

For example, if you think you hear a phone ringing while using a vacuum, then you turn the vacuum off to check, and you discover that the phone *is* ringing, that's a "subliminal programming" experience. Even though the sound of the vacuum was drowning out the ringing of the telephone (below your conscious perception), the actual ringing of the telephone prompted (or reinforced) your mental desire to take action and answer the call. There are different ways subliminal messages can be heard, one of which is to create and listen to your seven-minute PPM on your own.

Why Try Subliminal Messaging?

As previously mentioned, it's not just conscious thinking but *subconscious* thinking that holds the key to your life. I know this works; it has literally made me millions of dollars.

Many people believe the way their lives are is due to factors such as family background, education, economy, environment, fate, or simply pure luck. Ultimately, though, it's not outside circumstances that determine your life and make the difference between attaining happiness and success, or arriving at frustration and failure. The difference has to do with the beliefs, attitudes, thoughts, and behavior in the deep levels of your mind. This is in addition to the conscious thoughts that have made your life what it is today.

Outside influences may be what have prevented you from attaining your goals thus far. But you and your thoughts are your only limitations. Everyone's lives are what their thoughts and decisions have made. All of us are products of our own thinking. Subliminal programming will move you toward that which you desire. From now on, those old habits, behaviors, and beliefs can and will be replaced by the ones you plant and cultivate directly to your subconscious mind using your PPM. This will affect a conscious change, helping you to achieve your true potential.

Do you remember when we talked about all the negative messages we are bombarded with on a daily basis? Subliminal messaging, using your PPM, will allow you to access your subconscious mind, and change the effects of years of random messages received from the media, from friends, advertising, family, and colleagues. Following years of listening and accumulating this randomness, those messages have become embedded in your mind. These messages are responsible for causing your doubts and fears, as well as the habits you've formed which have the power to control the rest of your life, if you allow them to. These random messages can also prevent you from reaching your full and true potential.

There is one more way you can use your recording: sleep learning. I have done this and found that it works, especially if you want to turbo charge the change to your subconscious programming. Sleep learning works. Get a "pillow speaker" and have your seven-minute PPM play quietly and continuously while you sleep. This will send your PPM directly to your subconscious.

When I started out recording my PPM, I didn't have a laptop. In fact, I didn't have a computer at all. I was using a cassette recorder tape into which I had plugged a single earpiece. How times have changed! Now you can make this kind of recording on a Smartphone or a computer using free online recording programs, or iOS and android Apps for your Smartphone. You don't need any special software. I am only pointing out that it is available simple, free and easy.

You'll want to keep tabs on your progress and accomplishments as you begin to achieve your short-term and long-term goals. You will and should have goals that are three and six months from now.

These may be interim steps toward your larger goals. As such, it will become necessary to re-record as you progress and accomplish your goals. And you'll continue to set newer and higher goals, or maybe start adding in some goals you haven't even thought of yet.

Just remember that you don't want to make this recording too long. If it's fifteen minutes, you may start to make excuses not to listen to it because it seems too long as you get out of and/or get into bed. Keep it succinct and to the point. Everybody can take seven minutes just before they go to bed and as soon as they get up. It's powerful, and in my experience, it seems to work for everyone.

If one of your goals is to come up with ideas to create the wealth that you're after, then one of your tasks will be to come up with an idea, within the next three months, six months, or year, which you can implement almost immediately. This will assist you in creating the lifestyle that will enrich you in the ways you desire and provide you with the income you need. There are very few jobs that have the ability to create the lifestyle and freedom that you're likely after, but whether or not it's your dream job you're after, these strategies will work for you.

Maybe you simply want to increase your sales in your current job. These techniques work just as well for that scenario. The first year I employed this process in my real estate career, I doubled my sales. I was already "doing well," but I went from that to doing very, very well, and becoming one of the top 10 percent of realtors in my area. At the same time, as I was increasing my real estate sales, I was also creating a multi-million-dollar business.

Without any doubt, I can tell you that this process works. I've done it and I've seen it work for others. For these reasons, I can't encourage you strongly enough to take these simple techniques and utilize them. You will quickly discover what you need to do and can do in order to create the dreams that you're after. You will be able to create the success that you're after, create the lifestyle, the relationships, the fitness levels, and all of the goals that you're going to set out to accomplish. Whatever they are, you can achieve them by focusing on and utilizing your very own seven-minute PPM.

It's simple, and it's straightforward, but it is also amazingly powerful. It will work for you as it's worked for me. In the conclusion, we'll do a short review of what we've already covered. And I look forward to hearing the story of your success.

In literature and in life we ultimately pursue, not

conclusions, but beginnings.

Sam Tanenhaus

CONCLUSION

We've come a long way on our journey through this book, and during chapter ten, we put everything together. Now is the point when you should be ready to create your seven-minute Personal Programming Message. This message will be one of the most important things you've ever created in your life; it's going to help reprogram your subconscious mind.

Your PPM will also be responsible for changing you and helping you to become a goal magnet, who draws all the things that you envisage to you, who can have all the things you desire. You still have the choice to stay where you are and just continue working at what you're currently doing, but I know that you've decided to do what you've always dreamed of doing. By reading this book and getting this far, you've already made the important decision to change your life. Now it's up to you to put everything into action.

Anybody can do this. Everybody can access their subconscious minds and change their ability to attract the things that are important to them into their lives. In the same way you've created where you are *today*, you can go on to create something new for yourself, your future, and the future of your family. You can create new beginnings for yourself. By putting things into place and taking action, you will bring the laws of the universe onto your side and start to make things happen in your life in ways that you never thought were possible. It's all far easier than you ever imagined.

You can start slowly if you choose, but massive action is preferable because it sweeps you into momentum, giving you energy to build on and feed on. You're going to need the will to win, the strength to take action, and the conviction that your actions will manifest the changes you desire. That's what your Personal Programming Message will do for you. It helps keeps you focused on your goals and the tasks that will take you there.

Be honest with yourself, not only about where you are today, but also where you are in your progression. Don't worry if you have some setbacks along the way. Almost everybody does. Just learn from those moments, but also understand that there's only one way to fail, and that's to not take action at all.

Popular culture is full of songs and stories telling us that if we get knocked down, we should get up again. Remember, if you just get back on your feet one more time and keep going, you will always overcome, just as Calvin Coolidge said in the quote at the end of the book. I have had this quote stuck to my computer screen and desk for many, many years. Keep moving forward, keep envisioning your future, and keep programming your mind on a daily basis. Take seven minutes in the morning, fully relaxed, and seven minutes in the evening, just before you go to bed, and listen carefully to the words that you've created. Build your pictures and visions as you listen to your voice. Create a vision board of all you want to achieve. Feel the emotions that will reprogram your subconscious mind, and be sure to change your recording as you become more proficient at achieving your goals and continue to evolve.

It's important that we check ourselves on "what's the worst thing that could happen" by choosing to step out of our comfort zone, by choosing to change. Maybe you want to meet the person across the room, what's the worst that could happen if you choose to stand up and make your way over to meet them? What's the worst thing that could happen if you start a new part-time business from home that could make you a fortune down the road? What's truly the worst thing?

In reality, it's rare that you have anything to lose, in fact, and you have so much to gain, so be sure you take those chances. Step out and expand your comfort zone, even by taking only one step at a time. This is a process. "Rome wasn't built in a day," as the saying goes. It'll be a transition for you; it won't necessarily be an instant one. You may have some instant success, but this is a process of change. Remember that to form a new habit, it takes at least twenty-one days.

SIDE NOTES

I think it's important for you to continue to have fun and enjoy things in your life, just as you always have done. This transition toward your new future is an important one, but you need to have fun to make it all worthwhile. When you have some downtime, go see a comedy show, play a game, enjoy a walk in the park, or go to the beach. Do something that's invigorating and that affords you extra energy.

To gauge progress, you need to know where you are today. Take photos of wherever you go so you can look at them and understand where you've been. Enjoy these beautiful places on a daily basis as you go through your life. Look at the pictures, and think about how good it felt when they were taken. You now have an absolute roadmap for gaining the success that you're after, for changing your future in the ways you want to, and for making the alterations that you want to make. You still need to check your progress along the way. Find out where you are, where you're going, and whether you are making progress.

Learn to be an excellent communicator. Learn how to speak succinctly. Learn how to write well. These skills will help you immeasurably in all aspects of your life. As you articulate what you want in your life, your subconscious will achieve it, as long as you are clear, concise, and succinct about what it is you're after. People who can clearly articulate their objectives will often get a job over someone who cannot. You can choose to be an excellent communicator, or at least a better one. The ability to speak in front of people is an excellent attribute, and it will help you in so many ways, and in so many areas of your life.

Become the person you want to be. In other words, be that person now. Don't just read without taking action. You've gotten this far. It would be all too easy to go through this book saying, "Oh, I know that. I've read that before. I know that part." Without action, without putting in place the principles we've discussed, you won't achieve what you are after. By now, you should be building on your strengths. You should have made an assessment of your current assets. You should be building the picture of the future self you admire. By implementing the techniques in this book daily, repeatedly, and transforming your subconscious, you'll start to attract everything that you desire.

Keep studying. Continue to put these ideas and methods into practice. And keep coming up with new ideas. Be persistent and disciplined. Continue to train your brain to come up with new ideas to do what you're doing even better, to implement your strategies better, and to implement your plans better. Be prepared to do what it takes. Get right up each time you get knocked down.

So on that note, here are three short anecdotes about people who have persevered and really come out on top.

Did you know that Sylvester Stallone was rejected many times before he got the movie *Rocky* produced? Did you also know he was rejected 1,500 times before he was even able to get an agent in New York City? His life started out with enough difficulty as it was. Stallone was born with a condition that caused him to be paralyzed in the lower left side of his face. This is why he has such a unique expression and his trademark slurred speech. It is an affliction which presented many roadblocks that he clearly overcame with persistence. When he first went to New York City hoping to become an actor, he was turned down everywhere he went. No one wanted to hire him.

At one point in his life, Stallone slept in the New Jersey bus terminal for three weeks because he was completely broke. The only thing he still had was his beloved dog, which he was forced to sell to a stranger for money to buy food. It broke his heart, having to take that $25, and it was probably one of the lowest points in his life. His idea for the *Rocky* screenplay had come one day when he was watching Muhammad Ali in a boxing match. He wrote the script in three days. He eventually found someone who was willing to pay him $125,000 for the script, but the buyer didn't want Stallone to act in it. His self-belief was so strong that he walked away from the offer. This, despite being so broke and so down that he had been forced to sell his dog.

After a few weeks, the same company offered him $325,000 but still they didn't want him in the movie. Again, he refused. Eventually, he accepted an offer of only $35,000 because the company would allow him to take the lead role. When he got the money, the first thing he did was track down his beloved companion; he spent $15,000 tracing his dog and buying him back! Stallone ended up making $200 million from the *Rocky* movies, and the rest, as they say, is history.

Oprah Winfrey is said to have a net worth of almost three billion dollars, but it sure didn't start that way for the Hollywood superstar. She was born into abject poverty. She was the victim of rape at the age of nine and was pregnant at the age of fourteen. She later lost the baby in infancy. Things turned around for Oprah when she went to live with the person she calls her father. She started attending school regularly and got a radio gig during her high school years. By the age of nineteen she was co-anchoring a local evening news program, followed by her step into the daytime talk show arena. This and many other stories show that you can take charge of your life and make changes – big changes – if you really want to.

What about John Travolta? By the 1990s, he was virtually washed up as an actor, typecast into roles like the one he made famous in *Grease* (1978). That was until Quentin Tarantino cast him in *Pulp Fiction* (1994). From there, look at how Travolta's success skyrocketed, and look at where he is today. Wherever you've come from, whatever difficulties you've had, you can achieve greatness and great success.

The ideas in this book give you an exact methodology of what to do and how to do it. Read each section as many times as you need to in order to get the strategies firmly lodged in your brain. Go back over chapters as needed to help you get past any limits you may have had in the past and create an unlimited future for yourself. Whether you take the necessary action is up to you. You are the only boss of you. Remember that! You are the one who's in charge. You're the one who takes the definitive action and makes the decisions. To use a poker term, I suggest you go "all in."

MAKE IT HAPPEN AND MAKE IT HAPPEN FAST

Start now, putting everything you've learned into action, and you'll find great success coming your way. I'd also suggest finding a mentor. Choose someone you can identify with, who already enjoys success, and who has experience in the area you're interested in. Alternatively, find someone who wants to grow and learn with you.

Create a mastermind group of people with similar experiences or interests who all want to get ahead. On a weekly or monthly basis, talk about how each of your goals and objectives are manifesting themselves for you. Report to each other how things are progressing within your own lives, and enjoy listening to your peers and to stories of how well they are also doing.

You will all start to see things transform in your lives, and by working together as a group, you'll find that you can achieve many, many great things. The support that comes from being part of a mastermind group can be absolutely powerful as well. Having a mentor or a mastermind group can cut months or even years from the time it might otherwise take you to get where you want to go.

I feel strongly that this secondary suggestion is worthwhile. Sometimes somebody in the group will ask just the right question to trigger an idea in your mind. And it could be that idea that sets you on the path to your goal. Sometimes it's as simple as an old saying:

"Two heads are better than one," or "A problem shared is a problem halved." A different perspective on a problem or just another pair of eyes can clarify your thoughts and clear the road ahead for your continued progress. Talking to someone else can be a great help to both of you and your success.

I hope you've done all of the exercises found in the pages of this book, and that you've taken appropriate action on them, but if you haven't yet, go back and do the exercises now! Finish all the exercises so you can put your seven-minute Personal Programming Message together. It's that seven minutes of creation that will change your life. Again, I've done it, I know it in every aspect, and I know it works.

I strongly encourage you to do whatever you can to make it work for you too. You've got the power to transform your life now and forever. This is not a one-time thing, so as you continue to gain experience and success, as you change and continue to grow from where you currently are, be sure to upgrade your seven-minute PPM, your seven minute story to yourself.

In closing, I'll say this: take a risk that this will work for you. If you don't take action, or risk that is does work, there is of course no chance it will work! I am proof that these techniques work, and I've seen them work for many others.

I wish you all kinds of success in the future, and I look forward to hearing the stories of your success. As they say, "Today is the first day of the rest of your life." Make it the day you decided to take the action necessary to change your life and program your future into your subconscious.

APPENDIX A

This is a sample of the type of wording you should use when creating your seven-minute Personal Programming Message.

This script is not seven minutes in length; it is about two minutes long and is meant to serve as an example only. As you will see, it is written to evoke emotion for you and your subconscious mind. This example covers four areas: job, health, relationship, and a new business.

I should also add that, although this example is talking about meeting a special new person, your PPM can also be used to help make a current relationship even better. I will leave the wording to you, but with a thoughtful PPM, you can create whatever you are after.

Sample Personal Programming Messages

I am happy and healthy, and I look forward to every day with enthusiasm. Achieving all my goals and aspirations comes naturally and easily as I complete my daily tasks that are designed to attract everything I desire into my life.

I am earning a minimum of $100,000 in 20XX by making at least one sale per week. I enjoy making twenty cold calls every day, knowing that every call draws me closer to a sale and leads me to earning a minimum of $100,000 this year.

My cold calls and online campaign provide me with two sales presentation opportunities each week. I love doing my sales presentations in an upbeat and professional manner. I close one of every two presentations and receive referrals from my clients on a regular basis.

I am looking for a partner in my life who is X'X" tall, attractive, forward thinking, and has a positive zest for life. He (or she) is health conscious and loves going to the gym and to spin classes with me. I am open to finding this person wherever I might meet him (or her), and I send out positive energy letting the universe know I am open to meeting the right person.

I am fit and healthy. I love going to the gym a minimum of four times per week. I am energized by my two, hour-long spin classes and my two, hour-long strength and core classes. Each day I go, I increase my fitness and health in some way, and I feel better each time I go.

My XYZ part time business is thriving and growing each day. I spend a minimum of ten hours per week on my business. The more I tell people about what I am doing, the more I find people are interested in it and open to doing business with me. On my way to earning $100,000 per year I am earning a minimum of $X,000 per month by (month here) 31, 20XX.

In addition I own a new (choice of car) by the end of 20XX that my new XYZ business is paying for. It is metallic black, with a black leather interior, and navigation package, and it is fully loaded. That new car smell is amazing, and every time I see a (car brand), I want one even more.

You can of course go into even more detailed tasks, but I hope these examples inspire you and help understand the process even further.

APPENDIX B

THE EFFECT OF VARIABLES IN COMPOUNDING INVESTMENTS

TABLE 3. The Effect of Different Interest Rates on an Initial Investment of $1000, with an Addition of $200 per Month.

# Years	5%	6%	10%	11%	15%	20%
5	$14,941	$15,373	$17,262	$17,778	$20,044	$23,387
10	$32,833	$34,759	$44,017	$46,786	$60,172	$83,741
15	$55,794	$60,909	$88,039	$96,940	$144,728	$246,453
20	$85,262	$96,180	$160,467	$183,649	$322,906	$685,123
25	$123,079	$143,757	$279,635	$333,564	$698,359	$1,867,763
30	$171613	$207,930	$475,702	$592,753	$1,489,505	$5,056,126
35	$233,899	$294,490	$798,294	$1,040,871	$3,156,594	$13,651,851
40	$313,834	$411,247	$1,329,057	$1,815,626	$6,669,452	$36,825,674

TABLE 4. The Effect of Different Interest Rates on an Initial Investment of $100 with an Addition of $100 per Month

# Years	5%	6%	10%	11%	15%	20%
5	$6,957	$7,147	$7,973	$8,198	$9,178	$10,615
10	$15,758	$16,652	$20,926	$25,040	$29,310	$38,963
15	$27,052	$29,473	$42,238	$46,043	$68,622	$115,389
20	$41,546	$46,766	$77,303	$88,251	$153,567	$321,431
25	$60,147	$70,092	$134,995	$160,603	$332,562	$2,374,477
30	$84,019	$101,556	$150,397	$285,694	$1,504,511	$6,411,863
35	$114,656	$143,997	$386,092	$501,965	$1,504,511	$6,411,863
40	$153,974	$201,241	$643,048	$875,880	$3,179,246	$17,291,538

END NOTES

1. "Lottery win is retirement plan for 34% of poll respondents," CBC Business News, January 30, 2014, accessible at http://www.cbc.ca/news/business/lottery-win-is-retirement-plan-for-34-of-poll-respondents-1.2517046.

2. Tim Bowler, "Financial Investment Success: How Much Luck is Needed?" BBC Business News, April 30, 2014, accessible at http://www.bbc.com/news/business-27195861.

3. Ibid.

4. Alexandra Potter, *Be Careful What You Wish For* (Hodder, 2006)

5. See http://www.2knowmyself.com for various articles on this subject.

6. Jo Lewin, "10 foods to boost your brainpower," BBC Good Food, accessible at http://www.bbcgoodfood.com/howto/guide/10-foods-boost-your-brain-power.

7. Richard Wiseman, *The Telegraph*, January 9, 2003, accessible at http://www.telegraph.co.uk/technology/3304496/Be-lucky-its-an-easy-skill-to-learn.html

8. Lysann Damisch, Barbara Stoberock, and Thomas Mussweiler, "Keep Your Fingers Crossed! How Superstition Improves Performance" in *Psychological Science*, 21(7), pp 1014 –1020 (Association for Psychological Science, 2010) accessible at http://soco.uni-koeln.de/files/PsychS21_7.pdf

9. Michael Merzenich, *Soft Wired: How the New Science of Brain Plasticity Can Change Your Life* (Parnassus Publishing, 2013)

10. "The Law of Attraction – Ancient Egyptian Mirror Image Technique Discovery. Archeologist Reveals His Discovery Then Disappears!" October 23, 2010 accessible at http://masteryofself.wordpress.com/2010/10/23/the-law-of-attraction-ancient-egyptian-mirror-image-technique-discovery.

11. Stuart Wilde, *Little Money Bible: the Ten Laws of Abundance* (Hay House, 2001).

12. The Three Initiatives, *The Kybalion: A Study of The Hermetic Philosophy of Ancient Egypt and Greece* (Yogi Publication Society, 1908).

13. Elizabeth Landau, "The universe is expanding, but how quickly?" April 8, 2014, accessible at http://www.cnn.com/2014/04/08/tech/innovation/universe-expansion-astronomers/.

14. Bob Proctor, *The Science of Getting Rich: Using The Secret Law of Attraction to*

Accumulate Wealth (Seminars on DVD, 2004).

15. Michael Masterson, *The Pledge: Your Master Plan for an Abundant Life* (Wiley, 2010).

16. Mark Csabai, "Emotions and Brain Waves," accessible at http://victoriousliving.co.za/emotions-and-brain-waves/#more-177.

17. R. Morgan Griffin, "Periodontal Disease and Heart Health: Brushing and Flossing may Actually Save Your Life," accessible at http://www.webmd.com/heart-disease/features/periodontal-disease-heart-health

18. Aaron Gouveia, "2013 Wasting Time at Work Survey," accessible at http://www.salary.com/2013-wasting-time-at-work-survey/slide/2.

19. Ibid.

20. UCMAS Mental Math School, "Left Brain vs Right Brain," accessible at http://www.ucmas.ca/our-programs/whole-brain-development/left-brain-vs-right-brain.

21. Wikipedia entry for "Visual Thinking," accessible at http://en.wikipedia.org/wiki/Visual_thinking.

Be sure to visit the web site for free tips and reports on retiring rich, business ideas, creating wealth and more.

www.the7minutemillionaire.com

Nothing in this world can take the place of

persistence. Talent will not – nothing is more common

than unsuccessful men with talent. Genius will not –

unrewarded genius is almost a proverb. Education

will not – the world is full of educated derelicts.

Persistence and determination alone are omnipotent.

The slogan 'press on' has solved and always will solve

the problems of the human race.

Calvin Coolidge

ABOUT THE AUTHOR

Tony Neumeyer is a professional entrepreneur who has achieved remarkable success in numerous arenas, including real estate, nutrition, the stock market and more. Tony is also the publisher of *AmalgaTrader Magazine*, a digital magazine for traders and investors. Tony first employed the techniques offered in this book in the early 1990s to double his real estate sales in a single year, making him among the top realtors on the North Shore of Vancouver. He did this while simultaneously building a multi-million dollar direct marketing nutrition business and investing and speculating in the volatile market of small cap & penny stocks. Tony chose to write this book about the strategies he used and still uses to create his success, sure that others who chose to employ them can achieve the success they desire and strive for.

Be sure to visit the web site for free tips and reports on retiring rich, business ideas, creating wealth and more.

www.the7minutemillionaire.com

CPSIA information can be obtained at www.ICGtesting.com
Printed in the USA
LVOW07s1538120415

434255LV00001B/88/P